Hardening Your Macs

Keeping Apple Computers Safe at the Hardware and Software Level

Jesus Vigo, Jr.

Apress®

Hardening Your Macs: Keeping Apple Computers Safe at the Hardware and Software Level

Jesus Vigo, Jr.
Miami, FL, USA

ISBN-13 (pbk): 978-1-4842-8938-9   ISBN-13 (electronic): 978-1-4842-8939-6
https://doi.org/10.1007/978-1-4842-8939-6

Copyright © 2023 by Jesus Vigo, Jr.

Managing Director, Apress Media LLC: Welmoed Spahr
Acquisitions Editor: Susan McDermott
Development Editor: James Markham
Coordinating Editor: Jessica Vakili

Distributed to the book trade worldwide by Springer Science+Business Media New York, 233 Spring Street, 6th Floor, New York, NY 10013. Phone 1-800-SPRINGER, fax (201) 348-4505, e-mail orders-ny@springer-sbm.com, or visit www.springeronline.com. Apress Media, LLC is a California LLC and the sole member (owner) is Springer Science + Business Media Finance Inc (SSBM Finance Inc). SSBM Finance Inc is a **Delaware** corporation.

For information on translations, please e-mail booktranslations@springernature.com; for reprint, paperback, or audio rights, please e-mail bookpermissions@springernature.com.

Apress titles may be purchased in bulk for academic, corporate, or promotional use. eBook versions and licenses are also available for most titles. For more information, reference our Print and eBook Bulk Sales web page at http://www.apress.com/bulk-sales.

Any source code or other supplementary material referenced by the author in this book is available to readers on the Github repository: https://github.com/Apress/Hardening-Your-Macs. For more detailed information, please visit http://www.apress.com/source-code.

Printed on acid-free paper

To my gorgeous wife, Jackie – thank you for always believing in me and being a bright, shining light in my life.
—J.V.

Table of Contents

About the Author xi

About the Technical Reviewer xiii

Acknowledgments xv

Introduction xvii

Part I: Understanding Security 1

Chapter 1: Security 101 3

Introduction...4

What Is It? 6

Why Is It Important? 7

When Is It Necessary? 9

Who Is Responsible for It? 10

Summary...12

Chapter 2: Risky Business..13

Risk..14

Assessments..15

Matrix...18

Appetite..23

Tolerance..24

Summary...25

Chapter 3: A World of Hurt **27**

Threats 27

Attacks 31

Internal 33

External 37

Summary 40

Chapter 4: The Mind Stone **41**

Think Like Them 42

Act Like Them 45

Understand Them 47

Protect Against Them 49

Summary 50

Chapter 5: (Return of) the Mac **53**

macOS 55

Hardware 56

Software 57

Distribution 58

Frameworks 59

Security 60

Privacy 64

Summary 66

Part II: Welcome to the Rock **69**

Chapter 6: Lock It Down **71**

Hardening Process 71

Minimizing the Attack Surface 74

Identifying Vectors 75

Workarounds...77

Summary..80

Chapter 7: The Outer Limits 83

Startup 83

Volume-Level Encryption 86

Cable Lock 88

Sensor Covers 89

Accessories...90

Licensed Cables..93

Summary..94

Chapter 8: Inside Job...97

Passwords...97

Login 102

System Preferences...103

User Account Types...104

Multifactor Authentication...108

FileVault..110

Screen Saver...113

Lock Screen 115

Malware Protection..116

Firewall 119

VPN 122

Zero Trust 123

iCloud..126

Mac App Store...132

Secure Memory...134

Transparency, Consent and Control (TCC) 136

Touch ID 139

Software Update 141

Third-Party Patches 144

File and Folder Permissions 145

Sharing Preferences 156

System Integrity Protection (SIP) 166

Extensions 167

Time Machine 169

Remote Wipe 172

Summary 174

Part III: The Spoon Does Not Bend – Only Yourself 175

Chapter 9: Work Smarter, Not Harder 177

Remote Controlling Your Fleet 178

Mobile Device Management (MDM) 180

Device Configuration 183

App Deployment 185

Securing Devices 186

Automating Workflows 188

Zero Touch 189

Summary 192

Chapter 10: Have a Plan and Stick to It 193

Standardize Your Environment 194

Develop Workflows to Address Common Issues 196

Automate Whenever Possible 198

Stay on Top of the Latest Security Threats 199

Train Yourself (and Users) to Recognize Threats 202

Align with Security Frameworks 206

Comply with Regulatory Requirements..209

Design a Defense In-Depth Plan 211

Summary...216

Index 217

About the Author

Jesus Vigo, Jr. is currently the copywriter for security at Jamf. In a previous life before pivoting to writing, he held multiple IT roles during his career spanning over 25 years, beginning in the help desk role before holding several positions as a systems administrator and network administrator, ultimately moving toward managing all facets of the Apple ecosystem – supporting over 45,000 macOS & iOS-based devices – for one of the largest school districts in the United States. While this is the first book authored by Jesus, he has written for several industry periodicals, including blogs for TechRepublic covering security, tutorials, and best practices e-books with a uniquely Apple focus. Lastly, he also serves as a subject matter expert for CompTIA and a member of the CompTIA SME Technical Advisory Committee (CSTAC), providing support and expertise during the development of both high and low stakes certification exam development.

Jesus holds several technical certifications, over 30 in fact, ranging from several for device management from Apple and Jamf, with the large majority centering around security, including CompTIA Advanced Security Practitioner (CASP), PenTest+, and (ISC)^2 Systems Security Certified Practitioner (SSCP). He also holds a Bachelor of Science in Cybersecurity and Information Assurance from Western Governor's University.

About the Technical Reviewer

Steve Whalen is a Certified Computer Forensic Examiner (CFCE) with degrees in psychology and sociology and served as a Delaware State Trooper. As a state trooper, Steve worked as a detective with the Criminal Investigations Unit and served as their first full-time forensic examiner for digital evidence. Building off this experience, Steve helped the Delaware State Police develop its first High Technology Crimes Unit in 2001, where he processed thousands of electronic devices and media containing digital evidence from hundreds of cases relating to intrusion, financial crimes, child sexual exploitation, narcotics, stalking, and homicides.

After retiring from law enforcement, Steve co-founded SUMURI, a leading provider of hardware, software, training, and services relating to digital evidence and computer forensics worldwide. Steve was the designer of the successful Macintosh Forensic Survival Courses; RAPTOR, PALADIN, CARBON, and RECON forensic software; and TALINO workstations.

Steve has developed and delivered forensic training to thousands of investigators and examiners around the world through organizations such as the International Association of Computer Investigative Specialists (IACIS), the High Technology Crimes International Association (HTCIA), and the US Department of State Anti-Terrorism Assistance Program. Steve has over 20 years of experience in computer forensics and has provided training throughout North America, Asia, Europe, the Middle East, the Caribbean, Africa, and Oceania.

Wanting to do more, Steve founded the non-profit company Red Stapler Inc. and used his knowledge of digital forensics, psychology, and sociology to create a "first of its kind" software solution (catchapredator.org) to combat the sexual exploitation of children in a way that has never been done in all of history.

Acknowledgments

Security is a balancing act of not-so-equal parts art and science. The latter provides the necessary details to inform you of what's happening and what's affected, so that the issue can be addressed; the former, however, relies on your senses to feel out what you believe to be wrong, to be creative in looking for issues in the places where they aren't as obvious.

In other words, it's about judiciously mapping the data points about where a problem is identified while simultaneously being able to approach suspected issues with out-of-the-box thinking regarding solutions, when the data cannot be quantified or simply doesn't make sense.

Make no mistake, it takes years to hone your skills – much like it does when dealing with life's little curveballs. It helps to have an open mind and remain calm; after all, very few problems in life benefit by losing your cool, and computer security is definitely *not* one of them.

In my experience, I draw inspiration from many different sources, some for clarity, others for humor, and others still for perspective. Think of these as your totems, if you will. The things you turn to in life because they speak to you, almost guiding you. I'm grateful to the following for being my guiding principles: Buddha; Bruce Lee; meditation for philosophical points of view and helping to clear my mind when it gets too noisy around me; Stan Lee; Chris Claremont; David Michelini; Marv Wolfman and the creatives at Marvel and DC for providing me a much-needed respite at times and for helping me understand that life imitates art (or vice versa) and the course is not a straight line but a winding road; some of my favorite movies, like *Star Wars*, *The Godfather*, *Akira*, and *Pulp Fiction* – and their various creators – for the oh so helpful gut check and instilling in me the belief that looking at things from a different prism helps to reveal an answer you didn't quite know about or could even conceive.

Finally, I'd like to thank you – the reader – looking to expand your security knowledge base and taking the initiative to better secure your Apple computer, laptop, or the thousands of devices you're tasked with managing and keeping safeguarded.

Who This Book Is For

This book is for two types of audiences: consumers and IT administrators that are either new to the Apple ecosystem or those with several years of experience using a Mac under their belt. Regardless of the grouping in which you initially fall, you're all part of the same group of individuals that wish to better protect themselves, their data, and their privacy.

You will find this easy-to-follow guide invaluable in helping you to do just that when getting stuff done on your Mac computer, whether for work or pleasure – or both!

At the same time, IT administrators tasked with managing Mac will find nuggets of information within these pages to help them develop an information security policy that protects their device fleet from local and remote threats, while utilizing available security tools to lessen the administrative load that often comes with securing hundreds, thousands, or tens of thousands of macOS-based computers worldwide.

Introduction

Hardening your computing device(s) is one facet that administrators and users alike should consider within the greater context of securing your information. The hardening process, similar to the other processes that contribute to the overall holistic well-being of your device, is less about a single function that performs a specific action and more about a state of mind (as discussed previously). It is also coupled with relying on multiple facets working sequentially to achieve a desired state of security that mitigates or exceeds the level of tolerable risk.

In other words, a common belief held about security is the sense of a "one and done" or "silverbullet" solution that takes care of everything. A single solution that, once applied or installed, will magically protect your computer from every single threat (large or small) that comes your way.

At best, this is a misconception that comes back around to bite folks in the ass time and again through malware infections, network compromises, and/or theft of confidential data; at worst, it is a downright fallacy that could put your privacy and sensitive/confidential data at risk, alongside your financial and perhaps even physical well-being.

I do not share this to intimidate you with fear, uncertainty, and doubt (or FUD, as it's called), but rather to define two clear expectations before proceeding:

1. The above-mentioned risks as well as those contained in the following pages are based on real-world concerns. They may or may not apply to *your* specific situation, either in whole or in part, but just because something may not directly apply to you does not make that danger or threat any less credible, meaningful, or able to occur.

2. In this book, we will deal with hardening concepts relating to macOS only. While operating systems may share similarities like security concepts with one another, particularly the foundational ones that may be applicable in an overarching manner, the concepts and processes to minimize your Mac's attack surface make up just one aspect of a comprehensive defense-in-depth security plan, that is, it is not a "one and done" or "silverbullet" solution.

Chapters at a Glance

The book is split up into several chapters, each providing helpful insights into a specific theme, as well as tying into the larger, overarching theme of hardening your macOS computer. While I aim to be thorough and direct whenever possible, I often employ anecdotes or references that aid in explaining concepts, providing examples, and utilizing elements in a concerted effort to bridge gaps in knowledge, all in the service of forming a greater understanding between all the concepts shared throughout the book and how they tie into the larger security paradigm, in general.

Chapter 1: Security 101

The first chapter will answer the eternal question, "What is security?", using broad terminology to provide a foundational-level understanding as to why it is now more important than ever.

Chapter 2: Risky Business

Before any such security issues can be identified – and, subsequently, remediated – we need a clear understanding of what devices there are, how they're used, and what is the overall likelihood of them being attacked and compromised. Additionally, what the repercussions may be, should an exploited weakness lead to data loss.

Chapter 3: A World of Hurt

We crawl through the dark underbelly of computing, specifically the seemingly never-ending stream of threats and attacks that malicious actors leverage in order to gain access to macOS devices, by compromising security mechanisms with the ultimate aim of stealing data, eroding privacy, and, well, making good old-fashioned greenbacks from the sale, use, and/or ransom of the data our devices collect every second they're in use (and sometimes, even when they're not).

Chapter 4: The Mind Stone

Now that we've obtained some insight into how macOS works and the variety of threats and attacks that are used against them, let's delve into the mind of the attacker. More to the point, what are the motivations for executing attacks, how they're choosing their targets, and why they're attacking the Mac in the first place.

Chapter 5: (Return of) the Mac

While the Mac technically never left, the explosive growth in popularity has fueled its adoption rate as the consumer and enterprise device of choice. In this chapter, the differences that drive usage of the Mac by users will be discussed alongside how these differences change the approach to securing these devices.

Chapter 6: Lock It Down

By understanding the fundamentals of security, the need to fortify macOS comes into focus. Specifically, the term "hardening" refers to the process of configuring any vulnerable settings from their default state to a customized one to strengthen the security of a device.

Chapter 7: The Outer Limits

This chapter and the one that follows deal exclusively with hardening techniques to be used on your macOS device. Here, the features that pertain to or rely on hardware-specific components to be enabled securely will be discussed, including explaining what types of threats the solutions presented here protect against.

Chapter 8: Inside Job

Like the previous chapter, this one relates to software-based hardening techniques or, simply put, those that are configured directly within the macOS environment by a user or managed by an admin to further secure data from threats and attacks. It should be noted that the crux of the protections available is configured on the software side.

Chapter 9: Work Smarter, Not Harder

As a user, you likely only have one or two devices to worry about securing. IT admins, however, are often responsible for a significantly larger number of devices, any of which would only require one device to become compromised before it's game over. So, enterprise management requires additional tools that help IT manage all these devices with parity.

Chapter 10: Have a Plan and Stick to It

Now the time has come to put the knowledge and skills acquired into action. Not just to secure your devices, but to structure an ongoing plan that works to address your needs and that of your organization. Moving forward, standardizing a plan will aid in not only maintaining the security posture of your Apple devices, but also help fortify them against the latest threats, keeping devices as secure as possible while minimizing risk.

PART I

Understanding Security

Security is such a broad topic which spans philosophies, sets of principles, and procedures that are based on industry-backed best practices that could fill tomes. That is more than we could hope to possibly cover in a single book. However, this affords us the ability to focus in with laser precision on exactly what can be of best use to users and administrators alike, from a practical standpoint. In Part I of this book, we begin by grouping together the chapters that share common ground with respect to foundational concepts and basics for understanding security, threats and attacks, the risks involved, and the various components of your Mac that need protection.

CHAPTER 1

Security 101

In the 1995 hit anime movie *Ghost in the Shell*, the main protagonist who goes by the name of Matoko Kusanagi is a cyborg (half-human, half-robot) that finally comes to understand that her life's essence is greater than the vessel that contains it. Upon discovering this, she states "the net is vast and infinite," as part of this essence interfaces with the larger online world around her.

When thinking of security in this context, it's easy to feel overwhelmed by the sheer breadth of the myriad types of systems out in the world, the varying services they provide, how many users access them – both for legitimate and illegitimate reasons – and consider just how "safe" they may be. Adding additional chaos to those variables is the level of maintenance required to keep each of these devices operable and the myriad complexities are enough to scare anyone away from working in information security.

While at its core this is a book about computer security, it is limited to elements relating to securing your computer – not the world at large and every computing device on the Internet. Going back to the previous quote, I selected it to both explain in a primitive kind of way how, from a security point of view, all things are interconnected to some degree. At the same time, each person, business, and industry will focus, or rather should focus, on what they need to secure, taking steps to secure their resources, and not worrying about every single piece of protection out there, as it may have no direct impact on what you're trying to achieve.

© Jesus Vigo, Jr. 2023
J. Vigo, Jr., *Hardening Your Macs*, https://doi.org/10.1007/978-1-4842-8939-6_1

For example, if you're trying to protect your trusty MacBook Pro, a device that you take with you everywhere, get work done from there, do your schooling on it, watch Netflix from – basically, it's your "do everything" computer, and you want to make certain that if your device ever gets lost or stolen, no one but you will be able to access your private data, well, your focus should be on what can be done to tighten up the physical safeguards on your MacBook Pro itself, like using a strong password and enabling disk encryption, not necessarily worrying about whether you're safe when using a Wi-Fi hotspot.

It doesn't mean that you should arbitrarily use any Wi-Fi hotspot just because it's free and you need a stronger signal. Remember what I said earlier, everything is interconnected with security. But it does mean that learning about the different risks, assessing them for importance, and finally implementing them in a way that closes any loose ends is the best way to approach the personal security of your devices and data, and that's exactly what this book aims to do.

Introduction

Beginning with Part I, we cover the simple basics of security. Getting into understanding what it is, what it's not, why it's important, and who is responsible for it. After all, is it you? Did your job provide you a company-owned device, so is it their problem? Or is it Apple's?

Next, we dive into risk and what it means to determine which roadblocks lie in your path toward securing your device(s), as well as various types of ways to mitigate risk and resolve problems that would otherwise pose a threat to your device's security. The following two chapters discuss the different types of threats and attacks that exist "in the wild" – which is a euphemistic way of saying "online." It will provide a window into where these threats come from and, more importantly, give you an understanding of who are the ones on the other end of the attack. Questions like why they do it and how they do it will be discussed to give greater clarity into understanding the reasons behind the actions, ultimately shining a light on how to protect against them. As each chapter builds upon the previous, the culmination will lead to the various components that make up your Mac computer and how they fit into the larger framework of protecting yourself through hardening your Apple computer against everything discussed thus far.

Part II, while having decidedly less chapters than Part I, will contain the crux of the information regarding the hardening processes used to lockdown your Mac, including why it's necessary to be vigilant in identifying cracks in your Mac's armor and how to work around these issues when a proper solution isn't available. The two chapters that round out Part II are the "meat and potatoes" of this part, zeroing in specifically on the many hardware- and software-based protections that are available natively to macOS by Apple. Some of what we cover in this comprehensive part relates to identifying what should be secured, alongside the why and how they should be secured, to achieve maximum protection. You may be familiar with common factors, like having a strong password or making backups of your critical and important files, but did you know that even the strongest password can be bypassed if your Mac's not physically protected? Or how backups are seemingly worthless if you don't check them regularly to make sure that the data is being updated? Ask anyone who has ever faced losing important data who went on to restore from a backup they believed worked, only to find out the backup never *actually* saved their files correctly.

In Part III, we end on two chapters that are aimed more toward administrators, or those that have more than one device to take care of. Maybe you're an "unofficial IT person" for your relatives, or the one that's always solving your friend's computer problems wherever you go? Either way, Chapter 9 is all about "working smarter, *not* harder" – a mantra, if you will, that I developed earlier on in my IT career and have come to rely on it ever since. Not to be confused for being lazy, but rather borrowing more from the old engineering belief of "measure twice, cut once." In this case, working smarter refers to learning the ins and outs of your device(s), while marrying the requirements that are unique to your situation, to develop solutions that work to resolve your security concerns in as simplistic and easy to implement a manner as possible. The goal is not to reinvent the wheel, just to refine it so that it is customized to your needs so it can be used and reused time and again without having to go back to square one each time a problem comes up. Chapter 10 expands on the previous chapter with additional strategies to evolve your solutions, taking them to levels that are not only easy to perform and simple to implement but adaptable and extendable for multiple devices to be enhanced from a single solution source that continues to build upon the strong foundation established in Parts I and II.

What Is It?

security *noun*

    se·cu·ri·ty | \ si-'kyùr-ə-tē, -'kyər- \

    plural **securities**

    Definition of security

       1. the quality or state of being secure: such as

          a. freedom from danger

          b. freedom from fear or anxiety

          c. freedom from the prospect of being laid off

       2. something given, deposited, or pledged to make certain the fulfillment of an obligation

       3. an instrument of investment in the form of a document (such as a stock certificate or bond) providing evidence of its ownership

4. something that secures

    a. measures taken to guard against espionage or sabotage, crime, attack, or escape

    b. an organization or department whose task is security

As you can see from the preceding, the term security holds several meanings that parlay a specific significance depending on how it's used and intended. For the purposes of this book, we will focus on two of these meanings, 1a and 4a.

The former – 1a – relates to a more generalized sense of the word, think of this like a destination; while the latter – 4a – applies specifically to the various actions and tasks necessary to achieve said state of security. In other words, the path (4a) taken gets you to your destination (1a), with the path being any number of hardening tips provided in this book, making the destination where we want to be: a secure Mac that safeguards our data.

Why Is It Important?

Security wasn't always such a big deal. There was a time when users jumped on their computers when they needed to, whether it was for work or school, personal or pleasure – there was simply powering it on and getting to what you were doing – not passwords to remember, no secondary codes to authorize, or other such counter-productive interferences. This was also a time when users simply used the programs that were included with their computer's operating system.

In the case of macOS, or as it was known almost four decades ago when Apple first developed it in 1984, System Software, or Classic Mac OS contained within it several popular applications, such as a calculator, alarm clock, a sliding puzzle game, and the Note Pad app that allowed entered text to be saved onto your Floppy Disk (remember those?). These and several others were part of the desk accessories that came with the first version of Apple's OS, System 1 and allowed multiple versions to be used simultaneously, however, the caveat was only one application could run at a time.

So, you're probably thinking, why the history lesson? What does this have to do with why security is important? Well, I'm getting to that. It has everything to do with it, because security in those early days of computer design and software development was not a concern the designers or manufacturers felt was pertinent. There weren't any real-world causes for concern as Apple not only designed both its hardware and software to operate as one (much like it does now), but also, they were really the only ones designing software to run on these systems, as third-party developers were not something that would catch on until later years. Plus, computers were not relied upon so heavily as would end up becoming the situation decades later. Your social security number was placed on a card and given to you to store somewhere safe, like a safety deposit box, portable safe, or stuffed in an envelope under your mattress – but never your computer, because that was unheard of!

Also, computers in 1984 were very expensive, like thousands of dollars, so naturally not everyone had access to one, much less kept one in their homes. While the first *personal computer* (PC) may have been introduced back then, it wouldn't be until about the mid-1990s before computers would begin to gain the following that led them to be in people's homes, used for multiple tasks – both personal and professional – and really leveraged as business tools that gave rise to the modern-day uses.

More importantly, it was a combination of increased interest in personal computing, along with a real sense of concern surrounding computer security, with viruses and the fact that by the early 1990s, the few instances of viruses were contained to labs or on a single device, but now they were not only replicating but had found their way to people's computers at home.

With an evolving threat, the rise of broadband Internet's promise of a "fast and always on connection," adding to continued reliance on computers as mediums with which to edit, store, and distribute data, the once quaint and benevolent virus that would entertain users with a small poem or as a means to deter copywrite violations has grown to encompass multiple categories of threats across every single operating system on any device it runs on, targeting users personal and private details, company's sensitive data, highly classified government documents, banking details, social media platform access, gathering of location-based information to aid in stalking and human trafficking, the compromise of innumerable networks globally, the initialization of cyber warfare against countries, cyber terrorism, infringement of rights, such as free speech, civil liberties violations, and the list goes on and on.

Essentially any piece of data that is communicated over a device connected to the Internet, regardless of how trivial or inconsequential it may appear, is at risk of compromise and exposure, if not protected. That's why it's so important, because what started off as essentially a trivial matter has achieved critical mass, evolving into a business in its own right that is estimated to cost everyone – businesses and everyday regular folks alike – over $10 trillion dollars annually by 2025, according to IBM.

When Is It Necessary?

Would you believe me if I told you there was a time that folks would leave their homes or go to bed without locking the door to their home? It may sound far-fetched, but there too was a time when computer security was simply "not a thing."

While some would argue this to be a simpler time, regardless of where you stand on the issue, it's pretty safe to say that those times are nonexistent. In our modern world, one where virtually everything you do or say; work and play – regardless of how it's done – is processed to some degree on a computing device. What that entails is that ultimately, anything and everything is at risk at any given time.

So yes, in so many words, security is necessary all of the time. Think of it along the lines of paying car insurance for your vehicle. Maybe you're one of the lucky ones that's never been in a fender bender (or worse), so you don't have experience with what happens when you're involved in a car accident. While it's natural to ask yourself, "why do I need car insurance, when I've never even been in an accident?" The answer to this and likely any that questions the necessity of insurance is that you don't pay for insurance to avoid having accidents, you do so in the unlikely event that *you* do find yourself in one.

Security, in general, is sort of like that. You protect yourself against risks, or the potentiality of becoming a victim of a cybercrime...with the added benefit that, unlike the insurance referred to earlier, if the security you've configured is strong enough, it actually ***will*** keep you, your device, and your data safe from threats. And if you keep up with it, maintaining both it and your devices updated against the latest threats making their rounds, it will serve to fortify your system's defenses, also referred to as your **security posture**, providing continuous protection against current and future threats will minimize risk (which we'll dive into in Chapter 2).

Who Is Responsible for It?

Ah, the million-dollar question with an equal number of wrong answers and only a real handful of correct ones. Let me explain by breaking it down.

Before we start, we have to ask a preliminary question before we can begin to answer the main question. To determine responsibility, we ask is it a personal device owned by you or a company-owned device? If it's yours, well, then you're responsible. Congratulations! However, if it's a company-owned or enterprise device, then technically, it's still you that's responsible, but to a secondary degree. Primarily it's usually the responsibility of the company that issued you the device to protect their asset.

Back to the main question itself and why I refer to its value as a million dollars. That's straightforward to answer. Security threats that lead to a data breach, or what it's called when an attacker succeeds in stealing sensitive data from its target, cost $4.24 million dollars on average, according to cybersecurity statistics provided by CompTIA.

With average amounts that high, someone has to be held accountable for it. And that's where the answer to our preliminary question joins the spotlight. If it was your device that led to this breach, then you and you alone are responsible for it. If it's a company device, then they should have the right team of professionals in place to address threats and mitigate risk.

Either way, you as the user of the device have skin in the game too. After all, it is your data on the device, isn't it? If your work laptop gets compromised by malware that encrypts your private files and gives you 48 hours to pay $1,000 dollars for the decryption key, or else you'll never have access to your data again. Who does that hurt more, the company or you? Chances are likely that the company will simply erase your laptop and go on like business as usual; you, on the other hand, will be crushed to lose years of precious memories, financial documents, and other priceless data. So, at the end of the day, *you* too hold the responsibility to maintain the device you rely on daily as free from risk as possible.

The preceding of course does not represent every possible scenario. What really matters is what threat happens to target you. Meaning, if you keep passwords that are easy to guess or worse, keep one password for all your accounts, if a threat actor gets ahold of it, they could simultaneously wipe out your bank account, bad mouth your employer to get you fired, and besmirch your good name throughout all of social media putting you in a very tight jam. Unless your bank account happens to have over $4 million sitting there, personal damages won't be anywhere near the average enterprise-level damages mentioned previously. But the very real damage to your name and character could make it very difficult to obtain a job or make amends with friends and family while waiting for the bank to return your life savings.

If I'm painting a portrait of doom and gloom, my apologies. Like I mentioned before, it is not the intention of this book to play the role of scary Suzy, but rather to educate and provide practical solutions to protect you, those you care for, and/or those you're tasked with protecting. It just so happens that practicality requires real-world examples to bring the point home that it can get real bad, real quick and thus far what I've provided is rooted in real-world attacks that are unfortunately carried out each and every day.

Summary

In this chapter, I provided an introduction to basic computer security and explained what it is, while identifying what it is not. Additionally, we discussed why it is so important to safeguard our devices and data – even what it means for our personal safety – while also discussing how necessary it is, in this day and age of modern computing, when seemingly our entire lives are run through, or at the very least deeply enmeshed, with computers and the Internet at large, when everything is connected online, meaning the same "always open" door that allows posts to be liked, media to be shared, and messages to be sent also serves as the gateway for malware to infect your computer, invisible threats to stalk our every move, and our personal, most private moments to be made available for public consumption without our consent.

In simpler terms, risk, which will serve as the topic of Chapter 2, when we look at its various forms, discuss how to assess them, determine where our appetite levels lie, and how tolerance is best managed through the solutions provided in subsequent chapters.

CHAPTER 2

Risky Business

Before you can understand how to implement the proper strategies to protect something, you need to first know what exactly you're protecting, right? After all, what good is security if you apply the wrong solutions or forget to apply any protection whatsoever to certain devices?

This is where the concepts of risk, risk assessment, and risk matrices come into play by helping you break down what needs protecting and how to best protect it.

Additionally, the terms tolerance and appetite apply to risk-based concepts, helping you to determine not only which options are available to you, but to also pinpoint which one you're choosing to apply, based on the rationale behind why you've chosen a particular solution – even if the solution(s) chosen aren't necessarily the strongest or best.

You may be thinking, why would I go with one solution if a better one exists? It seems weird to not go with the best every time, but therein lies the rub as it were. Each piece of the risk assessment process helps you to identify which protections to use, discarding the others for various reasons which we'll dive into more in their respective sections. Just know that there's a method to the madness that will be explained as we wade deeper into risk-specific waters.

© Jesus Vigo, Jr. 2023
J. Vigo, Jr., *Hardening Your Macs*, https://doi.org/10.1007/978-1-4842-8939-6_2

Risk

Just what exactly is risk and what does it have to do with securing my Mac? Risk is, according to the Oxford Dictionary, "a situation involving exposure to danger." In the context of how it would apply to securing your Mac, risk is seen as anything that would cause threat or harm to your computer and/ or the data stored within it.

Consider risk as threats to your computer's security, like say the ransomware malware mentioned before that infects your computer and encrypts your data, forcing you to pay a hefty sum in order to regain access to your data, the bad actor sitting at your favorite coffee shop simply waiting for someone to leave their computer unattended so they can install a backdoor that will allow them to compromise your privacy remotely, or the message received from a "friend" on social media, containing a link to malicious code that pretends to require your credentials, all to obtain access to your accounts.

Each one of these risks present real threats that exist in the wild and are in use against an unknown number of targets every day. The goal with risk is to identify it, as many risk factors as possible in fact to better your assessment and keep the security of your device as strong as possible.

Something to know about risk – it cannot be fully eliminated. There is risk in everything we do in life; to a greater or lesser degree, it's always there. And so that extends to computing as well. Remember what I mentioned in Chapter 1 about "silver bullet" solutions – they don't exist – neither does a program or configuration that will work 100% of the time against a particular threat. Just continue to bear that in mind.

To know what risks are out there, I could simply tell you, but then this information would be outdated in such a short time anyways, since technology is ever-flowing. It evolves at such a frenetic pace that the safest bet is to stay on top of new and evolving threats by keeping oneself informed. Subscribe to security-focused websites to receive daily or weekly updates on the latest threats in the wild, keeping tabs of the latest updates for your device via software update notifications so you can keep software and hardware security at their maximum protection levels, and being proactive about security-focused reports in the news. All this helps to increase your security knowledge, in turn, providing you the level of awareness needed of the risks associated with your devices.

Assessments

While the preceding risk deals with the general types of security-related threats that exist in the real world, risk assessment, or simply the act of performing an assessment, is the next step in managing risk.

Here, an assessment's role is to analyze your device(s) to answer several specific questions that will aid you in determining what risks apply to you – and, subsequently, which do not – allowing you to develop a clearer understanding of the best route will be for protecting each device and help you to determine a plan to move forward in doing just that.

The following are some of the types of questions risk assessment seek to answer, to better inform you, the user or admin tasked with implementing the best level of protection for you and your device type(s):

- What are the different types of device(s) in use?

- How are these devices used?

- Who uses these devices?

- Where are these devices being used?

- What types of services and data are being accessed by the devices?

- Are those services managed by you or a third-party?

- Is that data stored locally on the device and/or on the cloud?

- The data that is accessed, how critical is it to you or the company you work for?

- If access to a device, data, or service was unavailable, how would that impact you or the company?

- If the device, data, or service was exposed publicly, how would that impact you or the company?

- Do you have any backups for devices, data, and services that suddenly become unavailable?

- How quickly would you or your company be able to get the backup device, data, or service operational?

- Is your industry regulated by any government laws?

- If so, what types of requirements do regulators impose on security protections that may affect your choices as a user or organization?

These are a lot of questions, I know. Sadly, this isn't the end of them either, as you'll find that often when the answers begin to roll in, they will change the context of, or introduce all new questions into the fray.

Before it all seems overwhelming, there is an upside and it is that these questions may only apply to you in part or not at all, depending on how you answer some of these questions. Particularly, the first seven. This is because, regardless of whether you're worried about your single MacBook Pro or you're an admin tasked with managing hundreds of them, the types of solutions that will be available will change, in some cases drastically, which all lead to filtering down to what will work best for you or your organization.

Part of that will of course center around cost, no doubt. Simply put, it's not going to cost the same for one license of say, consumer-level malware protection software for your personal MacBook Pro, then 100 or 1000 licenses of enterprise-level endpoint protection for a business.

And that's what lies at the core of performing a risk assessment, to determine what threats pose a risk to your device(s), how these threats affect you and would otherwise impact you if your device(s) became compromised, allowing you to search out solutions that will mitigate the risk in the best way possible with regards to your unique needs.

I also cannot stress enough the importance, I've found, of utilizing common sense when performing a risk assessment. It is too easy to get sucked into a paranoia state where we feel as though our devices are being tracked, that every glitch, such as a call drop or slow Internet is something far more nefarious working in the background to spy on us or steal our data. I'm not going to lie, as a security professional, you begin to develop that sense early on and that "negative view" only increases over time. Which is why I personally try to counter-balance it with common sense whenever possible. You just may find yourself "missing the forest for the trees" so to speak, thinking that the reason your device is operating sluggishly is because there is malware that is actively stealing the credentials to all your banking websites, when in fact, it's likely more attributable to the 30-plus tabs open on your browser, while running graphic design software to edit photographs, listening to music from the cloud, watching several tutorial videos in high-def, and keeping email, iMessage, and social media messenger apps open simultaneously. On a laptop with 8GB of RAM, you've far exceeded what the device can normally keep up with based on hardware specs alone, or what those in the IT industry affectionately refer to as "PEBKAC"; or *Problem Exists Between Keyboard And Chair*, aka the user is at fault.

Matrix

We're here to discuss the blockbuster movie with the ultimate hacker NEO, otherwise known as "The One", to save us all from the looming threat of robot overlords. (Hey, don't laugh, it could happen!)

Kidding aside, a matrix or matrices in the scope of risk refers to a table that is created by a user or admin that helps them to identify threats, the devices they wish to protect, and align the risk with the devices that pertain to them.

Again, this is one of those more advanced concepts that typically applies more to larger enterprise environments, much less so to individual users, but that's not to say that users won't benefit from writing it all out to visually identify what threats pose risk to their device(s). It will certainly help with the next phase in managing risk, Tolerance, but as mentioned previously, it's not exactly required.

The aim goes beyond just linking risk to device, but rather to include estimates on just how vulnerable devices are, how realistic the occurrence of the threat is, what sort of impact is expected if risk occurs, what the occurrence of that risk cost, and, finally, how much it would cost to remedy the risk before occurrence.

The following is a rudimentary example of a risk matrix for a MacBook Pro that personally belongs to a user and a second risk matrix for the same device, but being a corporate-owned device that is used by the same user. Someone that works remotely from home but does take the laptop everywhere they go to access social media websites for the latest memes and GIFs to share with friends. The hard drive is encrypted with a very strong, unique password.

Threat	Vulnerability	Impact	Likelihood	Risk	Control
Theft (Critical)	Loss of hardware. (High)	Access to work/ personal use unavailable until device is replaced. (Critical)	Device is taken outside of home (High)	Replacement MacBook Pro laptop costs $1,500. (Critical)	Do not remove the laptop from the user's home. Cost $0.
Malware Infection (Critical)	Malware modifies data. (High)	Loss of work/ personal data until restored. (Critical)	No malware protection installed on the device. (Critical)	Malware infection may delete, modify, or encrypt data, depending on infection type. Remediation cost depends on the type of infection and criticality of data. (Critical)	Install malware protection software with active scanning. Cost ranges from $0 to $100/ annually.

(continued)

Threat	Vulnerability	Impact	Likelihood	Risk	Control
Unsecure Wi-Fi Hotspot Usage (Critical)	Loss of data; Further compromise of accounts. (Critical)	Risk of eavesdropping to gather credentials and later attack/ compromise those accounts. (Critical)	Device connects to all Wi-Fi access without securing connection. (Critical)	Devices open to many attacks, including MitM, malware, phishing – all of which can lead to unknown losses. (Critical)	Do not connect to unknown/ untrusted Wi-Fi networks; or purchase VPN service to secure connection whenever in use. Cost averages $0–120/ annually.

(continued)

Threat	Vulnerability	Impact	Likelihood	Risk	Control
Theft (Critical)	Loss of hardware. (High)	Access to work use unavailable until device is replaced; loss of productivity could result in loss of revenue for the company until device is replaced. (Critical)	Device is taken outside of home office (High)	Replacement MacBook Pro laptop costs $1,500. (Critical)	Do not remove the laptop from the user's home office or invest in tracking software to increase the likelihood that the device will be returned or tracked down. Cost $0–60/per device per year.
Malware Infection (Critical)	Malware modifies data. (High)	Loss of work data until restored; Potential liability of exposure of sensitive, confidential data or trade secrets, which could cost the company in fines, litigation, and include bankruptcy and criminal prosecution. (Critical)	No endpoint security protection installed on the device. (Critical)	Malware infection may delete, modify, or encrypt data, depending on infection type. Remediation cost depends on the type of infection and criticality of data. (Critical)	Install endpoint security protection software with active scanning, compliance checking, and centralized reporting. Cost averages about $60/per device/ per year.

(continued)

Threat	Vulnerability	Impact	Likelihood	Risk	Control
Unsecure Wi-Fi Hotspot Usage (Critical)	Loss of data; Further compromise of enterprise accounts/ service, including lateral network compromise that could result in data breach. (Critical)	Risk of eavesdropping to gather credentials and later attack/ compromise those accounts. (Critical)	Device connects to all Wi-Fi access without securing connection or encrypting data in transit. (Critical)	Devices open to many attacks, including MitM, malware, phishing – all of which can lead to unknown losses. (Critical)	Implement policy-driven management that restricts connecting to unapproved Wi-Fi networks or implement ZTNA service that offers alwaysprotection to corporate-owned resources, by encrypting network connections and verifying device health prior to providing access to resources. Cost averages $0–60/per device/per year.

In glancing between both matrices, they are virtually identical up to the point of vulnerability, impact, and control. While the personal device has quite a few criticalities at stake, the fallout is generally limited to just the device/user itself.

While that doesn't mean there won't exist cases where it could be worse, the circumstances present themselves as much more dire in the company-owned matrix where the same behaviors could set events in motion that extend compromise to that of beyond the device and user itself. Leveraging the attack vectors presented here, a bad actor could do a major amount of damage without so much as ever even physically touching your device. By targeting the device over an unsecured network connection and phishing the user to click on a link, this is all it would take to result in installing malicious software that grants the attacker admin rights to the system, establishing a foundation for gathering intel, including credentials to enterprise resources, host names of other devices connecting to the same work-based networks, and an access path to the work network itself. From there, the attacker could potentially obtain many more devices to target, laterally compromising the entire network through the single doorway provided by your unsecured device.

This scenario presents a plausible example of how a relatively simple, yet common, fix could open the door to a larger-scale attack that could cost anyone associated – user or organization – any number of losses, and just how risks of all types, from low to critical, could be identified and mitigated through even the most basic of matrices.

Appetite

We're almost through the risk process. This section and the one that follows go somewhat hand-in-hand. They deal with the concepts of risk appetite and risk tolerance. We'll go more into the latter in the next section, but, for now, let's consider appetite as the amount of risk we're willing to generally accept; while tolerance represents how much we're willing to deviate from that acceptable risk in order to achieve a goal.

I'll use an analogy to explain. Being a Miami native, just about anyone that's lived in South Florida has made the 220-mile drive north to Orlando on at least one occasion. There's something about a mouse there that seems to be all the rage, but I digress. The most direct route is to take the Turnpike, which averages a speed of 60mph. So, if you do the math, the average time the trip takes is estimated at four hours. The 60mph posted speed limit could represent your appetite, as that's then a risk you wish to accept in order to minimize any trip-affecting issues, like getting into a fender bender or being issued a speeding citation.

Keep the preceding analogy in mind because we'll return to it shortly in the next section. For now, consider "appetite" to represent your capacity to assume risk. This quantifies what risk(s) you're comfortable in accepting.

Tolerance

As mentioned previously, tolerance and appetite go together. In this case, tolerance represents the limits of the risk we're willing to accept.

Returning to the Orlando analogy in the previous section, we determined that the posted speed limit of 60mph represents our risk appetite and will get us to our destination in roughly four hours. Now, say you've got a bit of a lead foot or simply just want to arrive in Orlando sooner, your appetite may be 60mph, but you realize that boosting your speed to 75mph will shave off almost an hour from your trip, bringing you closer to arriving within three hours vs. four.

In this scenario, your willingness to drive at faster speeds to get there sooner represents your tolerance. Or, how much more risk you're willing to shoulder to get there sooner. In this example, the additional risk comes in the form of driving 15mph above the posted speed limit, exchanging decreased safe driving with increased accident probability and greater chance of getting stopped by local law enforcement (which will not be cheap), all for arriving at your destination one hour sooner.

With the preceding in mind, we consider tolerance to represent the limits to the risk you're willing to accept in order to achieve a goal.

Summary

Armed with the knowledge on risk covered within this chapter, we now know that risk represents any possible threats to the security of your device. We discussed performing a risk assessment to determine what devices need protection, based on how they are used and what they are used for, in addition to other questions that help flesh out a more definitive answer.

Next, risk appetite and tolerance were discussed, providing insight into how one can determine what levels of risk are acceptable, which are not, and the limits of each. Gathering these data points alongside determination of risk factors and assessment information is invaluable when developing a matrix.

Lastly, the topic of creating a risk matrix was covered, as well as how it combines the potential risks and assessment information, coupled with the appetite and tolerance information, that help a user or an organization clearly outline what devices and services are in use to further determine what forms of protection will serve best at minimizing risk or effectively mitigating it, while addressing their unique security needs and concerns to keep device security as high as possible.

CHAPTER 3

A World of Hurt

Bad actors, no, not the kind that permeate Hollywood cinema. I'm referring to the ones that actively seek to invade your computing systems and network infrastructure in the hopes of breaching them to obtain sensitive and critical data. Another such term is threat actor. Both are used interchangeably and are synonymous with the more globally recognized term "hacker." Commonly known to the general masses as describing someone that steals something of value by attacking computer systems.

While we dive more deeply into the mind of a hacker in the next chapter, in this one, we delve into what I not-so-affectionately call, "a world of shit." Using the flowery descriptor to encompass the various threats and attacks – both internal and external – that the bad guys use in their malicious attempts to not only compromise devices but gather our personal, private, and sensitive data. As well as the motivation behind why they do this, providing a clearer picture as to what users and admins are up against when trying to keep devices and data protected against unauthorized access and invasion of privacy.

Threats

Threats come in all shapes and sizes. There's no two ways about it, anything can potentially be a threat – even something, such as an application that is secure today, could become compromised tomorrow (or may even be vulnerable right now, yet no one, not even the developer may even know). The point is, do everything in your power to ensure your

© Jesus Vigo, Jr. 2023
J. Vigo, Jr., *Hardening Your Macs*, https://doi.org/10.1007/978-1-4842-8939-6_3

devices are protected and data is safe, but don't let your guard down or allow yourself to fall into complacency, feeling as though you've nothing to worry about because that can all change in an instant....and once that occurs, there's seriously no telling how deep that rabbit hole could go.

In other words, always be vigilant. Information *is* your best friend in this case. One of the best sources of information relating to your Apple devices and software is the Apple website itself. Specifically, the Apple Security Updates site which is constantly being updated to reflect software fixes to known vulnerabilities recently discovered by Apple's security team and that of third-party security researchers that perform independent assessments of Apple hardware and software in the hopes of shaking loose any bugs that Apple developers may then patch.

Staying abreast of the latest updates is a great practice, especially when rolled into a patch management cadence that keeps your apps and devices up to date. But as far as threats go, vulnerabilities may take up a considerable amount of concern, but they are far from being the extent of the threats Apple users and admins will face unfortunately.

As mentioned before, threats come in all shapes and sizes, and from multiple different sources. What, where, when, why, how, and from who will vary greatly from person to person and organization. In other words, there is no, if you do this, then threat actors will target you with that. Anything and everything is a possibility when being targeted, so again, remain vigilant. With that said, certain types of threats are more likely to occur than others, given certain instances or situations.

For example, phishing is a common attack. Arguably, the most common attack vector in use today, preferred by threat actors for its ease of deployment, simplicity in execution, and considerably high success rate. The fact that it works against many users, regardless of whether they're sitting in a corporate office setting or working remotely, phishing campaigns can be adjusted to target any number of communication mediums, like email, SMS, social media, messaging, and telephone calls with little effort on the part of the attacker – yet the threat remains just as deadly.

Now take the same scenario, except that as a user, you do not utilize any of those forms of communication. I know, it's hard to conceive of this notion, but it exists – look at Christopher Walken, who chooses to eschew any computer-related usage, preferring face to face meetings. But I digress. A phishing campaign would not be terribly successful against someone like this because there is no simple way to reach the individual. Limited access = limited success. A threat actor could conceivably resort to mail correspondence or physically impersonating someone in a position of authority to get closer access to their target. The former seems like too much effort for no possibility of success; the latter, however, can and does work, albeit usually that places the threat actor at considerable risk of being caught, so it would likely occur against a corporate headquarters that requires physical access to the building and not as likely to be employed against a single user that doesn't communicate over the Internet much.

The point of the example is to consider threats in terms of probability or likelihood of occurrence, coupling that with the chances of success. Remember risk assessment? This is similar to that when determining which threats to prioritize your defenses against.

Another more simplified example. If you like to take your iPad everywhere and frequently work, study, or perform personal computing tasks from outside your home, then you're likely at a greater risk of device loss or theft due to the nature of working remotely so frequently. Considering a strong passcode and enabling biometrics, alongside a theft deterrent, like locking cable mechanism work to keep unauthorized users out of your device and deter stealing your fancy Apple iPad. Now, if you work only from home or at the office, the passcode/biometrics solution makes sense to ensure data privacy, but the security cable applies less. This doesn't mean your device can't be stolen if someone breaks into your home or the company's office, it just means that chances are less significant than if you travel everywhere with your iPad in tow.

We've covered a few threats thus far, but there is a great deal more. Too many to possibly cover in the scope of this book, but we will go over a few of the more common ones to better acclimate users and admins new to Mac.

- **Malware**: There are a variety of malware types, each offering a unique threat to your Mac. Some will spy on you, others will gather your files and upload them, while another will encrypt your data, then ask you to pay a ransom for the decryption key to restore access to your data or see it forever lost.

- **Eavesdropping**: Typically associated with open hotspots, the "free" Wi-Fi access is seldom truly free, but rather comes at the cost of exposing your device(s) to the Internet and anyone else that's currently connected to that unsecured wireless network as well.

- **Unauthorized access**: While we touched upon this in an example previously, unauthorized access doesn't necessarily mean someone reading through your email when you're not looking. It could also be someone rebooting your Mac to try to reset your password or adding a backup account for snooping later.

- **Rogue accessories**: This one has only gotten worse over time and will likely continue as we rely more on our devices and forget to carry our cables/chargers with us. These accessories have been known to be tampered with, having a means of intercepting data transfers and routing them to other devices or recording it to memory. Have you considered if that charging station open to the public isn't connected to a minicomputer on the other end, scrapping your files and collecting your precious data? How would you know?

- **Potentially unwanted apps**: Just because there's an app for everything doesn't mean you should download them all. This isn't Pokémon, and some of these apps, seemingly benign, could be secretly tracking your movements, copying your pictures, or granting the developer access to stored recordings, like conversations over the microphone or chat logs.

- **Suspicious websites**: Admittedly, this one is difficult to quantify. Just because a site is suspect, does not make it compromised. But the adage remains, if it's too good to be true, it probably is. Visiting questionable websites has a history almost as long as the Internet itself, just remember that this, like phishing, is also low hanging fruit for threat actors. Only in this case, the prey brings themself to the predator.

Attacks

If a threat is like a verbal insult, then an attack is akin to getting punched in the gut, poked in the eye, or kneed in the groin. They are multiple, and they target different parts and can be combined to cause major damage.

In computer security, malicious actors have a wealth of attacks at their disposal. And depending on what they seek to achieve, and the varying levels of security employed (or not employed), chances are great that they've got at least a few attacks that they can combine to whittle down your device's defenses, slowly eroding any security in place before finally being able to access what they came for.

It should be noted that the major difference between threats and attacks is as follows:

- **Threats**: Categorized by type, threats identify the potential issues that could affect a computing device, if exploited.

- **Attacks**: Classified by criticality, attacks are the act of exploiting a concern or issue on a computing device, causing a disruption to its normal operating procedure.

And like threats, identifying each and every attack could result in having a book written detailing each of those which is beyond the scope of this particular book. However, we will cover a number of different attack types, specifying between internal and external attacks, explain why they're used by bad actors, how they work, and what is targeted by each of the attacks we'll discuss.

Before we get into the attacks themselves, let's review some of the types of categories that attacks fall into, grouped by the parts of the system they primarily target:

- **Hardware**: Attacking the physical device, be it a MacBook, iMac, iPad, or iPhone, these types of attacks typically rely on physical access to the device. Exploiting open USB/Lightning ports, missing firmware passwords or gaining access to internal components, like the HDD/SSD and RAM.

- **Software**: Software-based attacks can occur locally or remotely, depending on the attack. They usually target weak or missing passwords, installing rogue/compromised/unpatched apps and running malicious code that allows greater access to the device and hardware-based resources, like stored data and the webcam.

- **Network**: Like software-based ones, network attacks rely on the software component as the vector to obtain access to the device remotely, acquire access to web-based apps and services or listen in on communications that occur over network connections, like SMS, chat, and email.

- **User**: The grail of attacks, user-based ones target – wait for it – users. What's the sense in spending countless hours researching and deploying highly technical attacks against a Mac or iPhone when all it takes is one cleverly sent text message or email for a user to simply hand over the keys to the kingdom (i.e., their logon credentials)? The majority of these attacks focus on social engineering or preying on a user's good nature to obtain information, data, and/or access to a system through deception.

In the next two sections, we dive deeper into the attacks themselves and identify whether they are internal or external attack types.

Internal

For the purposes of making attacks simpler to comprehend, we're splitting them into two sub-categories: internal and external. Internal attacks are types that typically occur from within the system, or put another way, by those that have already been granted access to the device itself.

This doesn't mean to infer that anyone performing an internal attack is guilty of being a bad actor, per se. Just that there is an equal possibility that the act being performed could be malicious in nature or simply carried out by someone that didn't know. In these instances, the intention of the agent makes all the difference between someone meaning to cause harm and those that are merely collateral damage of the targeted attack.

One last thing to note, this categorical breakdown is by no means exclusive. Meaning that, attacks designated as "internal" can't only occur internally, nor can attacks designated as "external" only occur externally. As you'll notice among some of the attack types, they are designed in such a way as to lend themselves to both internal and external – only depending on how it is being deployed to discern itself as one type over the other. Usually, bad actors will do this to maximize the success rate of the attack, based on the vectors available to them to carry out the attack.

- **Insider threats**: An insider is often a user that has been granted access to a device, system, service, or application by the organization or an administrator. Think employees, contractors – basically anyone that has a legitimate reason to access resources and has been authorized to do so. The threat here stems from a user that may be abusing the authorization they've been provided to perform an attack and/or commit a crime. Examples of insider threats are, stealing confidential data for financial or another form of gain, leveraging access to cause harm to or damage the organization, or malicious destruction of data and/or infrastructure, also in concert with causing damage.

- **Data exfiltration (local)**: Similar to the preceding insider threat, exfiltrating data locally requires a source that has access to the system/data in question, often copying the data to a USB Flash Drive or cloud-based service, to perform unauthorized distribution, sale, or destroying the original source of the data for monetary gain or revenge.

- **Man-in-the-middle (MitM)**: This attack is a popular one that is carried out frequently anywhere free Wi-Fi is available. Whether tricking visitors into connecting to nearly identically named hotspots or convincing them to visit compromised websites, threat actors can position themselves between the victim and their incoming/outgoing communications, effectively eavesdropping on unencrypted sessions, including accessing any data transferred/received.

- **Theft/loss**: Not specific to computer security, but certainly an easy way to gain access to unauthorized systems and data through theft. With devices getting lighter and thinner, it takes all of three seconds to fold a laptop or tablet into a bag or simply walk out with it without being seen.

- **Modifying configurations**: More complex, but harder to detect. Changing configurations yourself (or someone making a change without your consent), like creating a backdoor account or enabling file sharing can open a hole in your device's security that you may not even be aware of until it's too late.

- **Disabled settings**: Like the previous modifying configurations, disabling known settings can also leave devices unprotected. For example, an employee disabling endpoint security because it slows down the computer's performance is not uncommon and can put the device, its data, or your whole organization at risk of compromise.

- **Shadow IT**: Speaking of risk, shadow IT opens organizations to any number of security, compliance, and/or legal liabilities through the use of unsanctioned apps and services that may not have the same level of security as supported apps.

- **Shoulder surfing**: Casually glancing at a user's device while they enter their password or use a passcode to unlock their device is not only rude and unprofessional, it requires little effort, with the payoff of accessing someone else's account with all the rights and privileges assigned to it.

- **Unauthorized device usage**: Like shadow IT, using unauthorized devices may or may not be done maliciously, but the results invariably end up the same: sensitive data is now stored on an untrusted device that may not have endpoint security enabled, leading to exfiltration, exploitation of vulnerabilities, and/or full-bore data breach…and it wouldn't be the first time.

- **Social engineering (local)**: Saving the best for last, social engineering by, say, having a casual conversation with a colleague or someone you just met could result in inadvertently releasing details that include or can provide insight into your credentials, what websites you visit, where you do your banking, and so forth, providing the bad actor with all the details they need to successfully compromise your device and data, without ever resorting to sophisticated hacking tools.

External

Attacks in this section are placed under the external category, or those that typically occur remotely and do not require direct, physical access to a device.

As mentioned previously, external attacks are not mutually exclusive, as many of these can be executed from an internal source to some extent. But simply put, external attacks can be executed and carried out over a network connection, often occurring in the background without the end-user knowing and leaving behind very few Indicators of Compromise (IoC), as it's referred to, when "digital evidence" that an attack has been performed (or is currently happening) exists on the victim's device.

- **Malware**: Whether it's a virus or variant, trojan, or simply a potentially unwanted application, the malicious code that runs when one of these types of malware apps is executed could lead to anything from spying on your online behaviors to encrypting your files in exchange for a ransom to actively using your device to track your every move via GPS, recording conversations and sending copies of pictures to someone that may be stalking you or a loved one.

- **Data exfiltration (remote)**: Just like the internal version, remote data exfiltration occurs when software executes on your device that scans for certain types of files or hardcoded directories and uploads their contents back to an attacker or shares it online without authorization.

- **Vulnerability/exploit**: Vulnerabilities can exist within any system, app, or service; exploits are the result of a vulnerability that is not fixed, patched, or updated that – if left uncorrected – provides an attacker a path into your device, often allowing them to access your data or to take over control of the system completely.

- **Phishing (variations)**: Whether you're receiving an unsolicited email, SMS, telephone call, or message on social media or a chat app that pertains to requesting you to change your password, provide financial details, or threaten you with some form of jail time, chances are it's a scam.

- **Unauthorized access**: Accessing another device without authorization is a federal crime. That said, any form of unauthorized access, regardless of whether it stems from extensive security research or simply the user forgetting to change the default password, does not make it any less illegal, but the perceived veil of anonymity from remotely trying provides greater stealth for actors while not signaling to victims.

- **Denial of service (DoS)**: Essentially, disabling a service or access to a service by exploiting a system's natural limitations. Such as turning a computer off and on repeatedly until the power supply blows a fuse, preventing anyone else from using that computer. A variation of this is the Distributed Denial of Service (DDoS), when multiple computers are employed at the same time to bring down a service.

- **Web**: Web-based in this context refers to attacks against servers hosting services and apps. Your own Mac could be hosting a server, like a private website that attackers may probe remotely to obtain information to better attack it. For example, seeing if the hosting software is outdated.

- **Password**: One of the most common types of attack are those against your password. From simply guessing to leveraging computers to try lists of commonly used passwords in an attempt to brute force access to your device. Another reason why strong, unique passwords are recommended; and why you should *always* change the default password.

- **SQL injection**: Databases use a programming language to manage data. One of the more common languages is Structured Query Language, or SQL for short. Unfortunately, SQL isn't too difficult to learn and that makes it incredibly easy to obtain information from when the databases are not fortified. This ease also extends to manipulating data, easily allowing data sets to be changed, poisoning results with a few keystrokes.

- **Social engineering (remote)**: Once again, we're back to social engineering. While the attack results in actors obtaining the same types of information, the methods deployed are far better at obscuring an attacker. Such as email phishing campaigns, calling your phone and pretending to be a representative from a company you're a customer of, or contacting you via your computer itself in order to convince you to divulge your credentials or authorize remote access to "fix the virus on your computer."

39

Summary

In this chapter, I discussed what threats and attacks are and how they differ. Also, I explained how internal and external attacks – though similar in how they attempt to compromise your devices and sensitive data – go about doing so in sometimes very different ways.

Lastly, several different types of attacks were highlighted and explained, as well as categorized between being launched internally by someone with physical access to a system; or externally, executed by a threat actor over a network connection, like Wi-Fi or cellular, along with their subtle differences, including explaining the context behind why certain attacks are used, when, and against only certain types of services and applications.

CHAPTER 4

The Mind Stone

In this chapter, we're going to pivot ever so slightly, changing gears from the previous chapter that was focused more on threats and attack types to that of the attackers themselves. To further understand computer security and by extension, protect your Mac from current and surprisingly novel ways that bad actors continue to develop to attack macOS-based devices, one should try to see things as they do.

Now I'm not suggesting you quit your day job and seek a position in Information Security (though, if you were inclined to make a career jump, now's the time to do it, with the global shortage of cybersecurity professionals and all). But rather, by developing the mindset of a threat actor, you can not only get a sense of how they think but also how they act when opportunities arise. Armed with that knowledge, you can gain a better understanding of threat actors and their mindset, in turn allowing you to better protect yourself against potential threats and future attacks.

As the saying goes, "*scientia potentia est*." Translated from Latin and better known as "knowledge is power." But bear in mind that while obtaining the knowledge is great, as far as this book is concerned, that's only half the battle. The other half is applying this newly gained perception to your personal and/or professional situation(s) to truly reap the benefits of protecting your devices and sensitive data.

Power without perception is virtually useless and therefore of no true value! —*Ryuken*, Fist of the North Star

© Jesus Vigo, Jr. 2023
J. Vigo, Jr., *Hardening Your Macs*, https://doi.org/10.1007/978-1-4842-8939-6_4

The bridging of perception and power in this case forms the crux of where your security understanding intersects with implementing the procedures that will secure your devices today, while adapting protection into the future.

Think Like Them

I know this is a tough ask. Especially for those that have little to no experience managing Apple devices beyond making sure they don't leave their iPhone behind or that your MacBook Pro doesn't get stolen. But believe it or not, you're already on the right track if your mind tends to go in that direction when you take your MacBook Pro out of the safe confines of your home or office.

What I am saying is that, thinking like a "hacker" doesn't mean "be an expert in all things cybersecurity." Instead, what I'm asking you to do is to take a moment to think about your actions *before* doing them and to consider the consequences that doing or not doing something *could* render.

I'm going to use taking your MacBook Pro to your local coffee shop as an example. You walk into the shop and queue up in line to place your order and pay for your favorite drink. You decide to grab a small table and seat near the door, since there are a lot of other patrons in there working, studying or passing the time as well.

You set yourself up, laptop is out and open, connected to the power outlet and Wi-Fi. As you start to login to the portal at work, the barista calls your name. You get up to retrieve your coffee, then head over to the small table to add more cream and sugar to get it just right before setting the drink down and heading to the restroom before finally diving into your work tasks.

At the outset, it seems pretty straightforward, no? Just hanging out at the coffee house to grab a quick drink as you settle in to get some work accomplished. From my perspective, I identified the following seven instances where a bad actor could have potentially wrecked your day before it even had a chance to start with a few security threats:

1. You left your laptop unlocked when you weren't around.

2. You connected to (unsecure) public Wi-Fi.

3. You logged in to work, with access to work-related data accessible.

4. You left your laptop unattended several times.

5. An attacker could eavesdrop on your wireless connection since it's not secured.

6. An attacker could install malware and/or exfiltrate (copied) work and/or personal data from your computer.

7. A thief could simply grab your laptop on the way out the door.

In this scenario, you had complete control over each action that occurred. Meaning, had you modified each action somewhat, the outcome would be different, allowing them to be secured in the process. Let me explain by changing up the example.

You set yourself up, laptop is out and open, connected to the power outlet, security cable and Wi-Fi. You also connect to VPN. As you start to login to the portal at work, the barista calls your name. You lock your computer before getting up to retrieve your coffee, then head over to the small table to add more cream and sugar to get it just right. As you set the drink down, you disconnect your laptop and take it with you as you head to the restroom before finally diving into your work tasks.

Is it as easy and carefree as the previous example? Nope. Does it require more from you as a user? Absolutely. Is it a pain to have to execute so many extra steps? Maybe, that's subjective. But the most important question, is it safer? You know it!

See, when comparing the two scenarios, the latter:

1. Keep your laptop locked when you aren't around.

2. You connected to VPN, securing the insecure Wi-Fi connection.

3. You logged in to work, but access to work-related data was inaccessible (because your laptop was locked).

4. You left your laptop locked with a security cable, deterring theft.

5. An attacker could **not** eavesdrop on your wireless connection since it's not secured.

6. An attacker could **not** install malware and/or exfiltrate (copied) work and/or personal data from your computer.

7. A thief could **not** simply grab your laptop on the way out the door because you took it with you while in the restroom.

In a nutshell, it really comes down to cause and effect. If this, then that. While I'm not trying to trivialize this in any way, the basic gist extends into other security-based concerns. Such as, downloading software from a known developer's website or the trusted Mac App Store vs. a website that is advertising it as a "free" download or from a friend you've never met that claims to have found it online.

It's okay if you can't think of all the variables in a situation because you don't really need to. The aim of thinking in this mindset is truly to identify the right course of action (or if unsure what that might be), stick to the one that represents the least amount of risk, so that you maximize the security posture of your device for the greatest level of protection.

When combining the mindset with the other skills in the chapter, and the information gained by staying abreast of the newest threats, that combination of knowledge truly represents power. Which is further channeled by leveraging that to make good decisions regarding the safety and security of yourself and your device(s).

Act Like Them

DISCLAIMER: DO NOT ATTEMPT TO ATTACK ANY DEVICE THAT DOES NOT BELONG TO YOU. ADDITIONALLY, DO NOT TRESPASS ON A NETWORK THAT YOU ARE NOT AUTHORIZED TO ACCESS, OR OTHERWISE ATTEMPT TO CIRCUMVENT OR "TEST" THEIR LEVEL OF SECURITY.

THESE ACTIONS MAY BE ILLEGAL IN YOUR REGION AND MAY RESULT IN PENALTIES INCLUDING CIVIL AND/OR CRIMINAL ACTIONS AGAINST YOU.

YOU'VE BEEN WARNED!

Just a small disclaimer that explicitly states that I do not condone circumvention of security controls on any system that you – the user or admin – do not rightfully own or are authorized upon which to do so.

When I use the word "act" like them, I do not mean to go out and break the laws of your country or region pertaining to computer security. Let that be clear.

What I do mean is to act as though you are aware of the variety of computer security threats that exist out there, using that insight to protect yourself online and your devices accordingly. How do you do that, you ask. By mentally practicing the skills you've developed in thinking like them, using them to identify potential issues in how you conduct yourself that may otherwise lead you to becoming a victim if not corrected.

In the previous section, we used the example of an employee working remotely from a neighborhood coffee house. Perhaps the next time you find yourself working remotely just like the user in the example, take a moment to assess yourself and the actions you take. Are you performing any actions that could lead to becoming a victim? If so, there's an excellent opportunity to develop your own workflow to better protect yourself.

If you don't know or maybe you're too biased to really assess yourself, that's ok. Like any skill, it's one that will develop stronger as you put in the work. For starters, maybe try to spot the behaviors in others, like people watching. Watching closely for signs of actions that could be used against them to compromise their devices and/or data.

Don't act on it. It's all fun and games until someone goes to prison. And make no mistake, many computer-based crimes are felony class violations, making them offenses punishable by prison sentences, so look, but don't touch, ok?

A useful tactic is to spot these situations occurring, then come up with solutions to them. This helps to really build the cognitive associations between the "bad" behavior and the "right" action to take. Over time, you will find yourself only performing the corrective behaviors through practice, not unlike how we learn the right way to do something after doing incorrectly. The period of time will vary from person to person, but eventually the corrected action becomes a learned habit.

For those with an adventurous spirit or perhaps those that learn by working on something hands-on, researching, and staying informed on the latest threat trends is part of the solution. The other is performing them yourself. After all, the best way to know how to fix something is to be able to break it and put it back together again, I say.

These types of actions are typically aimed more at admins looking for ways to test out the theory. By putting into practice what they've learned, they can not only figure out how to do things the right way, but because computer security varies from organization to organization, by testing practices first, newer, potentially better ways may be identified that provide greater levels of protection that address the unique needs of your organization.

Best practices exist for a reason, but any admin worth their salt will admit that you don't implement anything into production until you've had a chance to test it for yourself to see how it will respond to your environment. While theoretically it may work one way on a Mac, the moment you push that solution to 1000 different Macs, something entirely different could occur on your network, so you always want to be as prepared as possible.

Understand Them

Over time, the process of thinking like and understanding how bad actors operate will give way to understanding what drives them…at least partially.

There are a variety of reasons why individuals turn to hacking. Some do so for the sheer joy of being able to circumvent security systems, while others do so for profit. Typically, the latter are considered more criminal in nature, but to provide greater clarity into the different types of motivations for hacking, here's a list, including what primarily drives each group:

- Black hats: "The bad guys," as it were. These individuals typically are very knowledgeable in computer security and use their skills to attack organizations for profit. Whether the target is harassed and/or the data stolen is sold to the highest bidder on the dark web – most of the time – the clear aim is to enrich themselves by illegal means.

- White hats: "The good guys." In contrast to the preceding black hats, white hats hold similar skills in computer security; however, these individuals choose to use their power for good, by providing services to organizations that will test out their security protection to identify any weaknesses before the bad guys do. It should be noted that white hats operate within the parameters of the law and are authorized by the companies that employ them to perform hacking tasks.

- Grey hats: Falling somewhere in the middle between the good and bad guys, grey hats don't have a particular predetermined agenda. Instead, they are typically driven by pure interest in computer security and attempting to circumvent protections or find loopholes for the fun of it.

- Script kiddies: Considered the newbies of the security world, this group of individuals may hold some knowledge of computer security, but generally rely on the pre-packaged work done by other, more experienced hackers to attack websites and organizations.

- Nation-State/Sponsored: This group of security experts is employed by a nation or country, often employing their skills at cracking security systems and developing malware that attacks specific targets. Their aim is to acquire sensitive data about other countries, especially if they represent a danger to the nation or country's sovereignty.

- Hacktivist: Think of activists and how they protest inequalities or unfair practices, except instead of picket signs and sit-ins, this group uses their expertise in cybersecurity to attack websites and networks belonging to organizations and/or governments to highlight their cause and bring about change or justice.

- Whistleblower: This group does not necessarily have to be a security expert, but it often helps aid their mission of gathering and releasing data anonymously, with the intent to expose wrongdoing, including illegal activities or cover-ups by an organization, government, or ally.

There are other types of motivating factors, and no group is specifically tied to their primary motivation. After all, all it takes for a white hat to become a black hat is to simply attack a system without authorization or a hacktivist to get paid by a random country for their work or to be sponsored by a nation-state.

More importantly, this insight adds color to why the various types of attacks exist and how they might be used by different groupings of bad actors to target you personally, the company you work for, or the systems you're tasked with protecting as an admin.

Protect Against Them

For the final part of this chapter, we combine all the components of thinking, acting, and understanding the mentality and motivation of a bad actor, using that converged knowledge to better protect our devices, our data, and ourselves against threats and attacks.

Consider, for example, the following scenario. You are an employee for ACME products, leading purveyor of low-cost goods made from questionable and very hazardous materials. While you are an associate and far from the CEO of the company, your employment with ACME is enough to warrant taking extra precautions to protect yourself and your device from security threats, particularly those that may seem innocent enough, like requests on social media or SMS messages from individuals you do not know.

These types of threats could be honest mistakes on behalf of the sender, or they could be seen as "dipping a toe into the water," or a method of checking if you're prone to clicking on the link threat actors might send you as part of a stepping stone on the path to a larger attack against your employer.

Similarly, utilizing the same scenario, but this time you are the CEO of ACME products, well, another bullseye has been added to your back then. See, the previously mentioned threats are still very real, but your elevated status in the company now provides bad actors the motivation that – as CEO – you are privy to a higher classification of information. This information could be confidential data about products, hazardous waste materials used in the development of ACME products, or even less-than-legal methods of waste management.

Either way, whereas before the employee only had black hats and script kiddies to worry about, the CEO has those threats in addition to hacktivists and perhaps even nation-states joining the potential threats to computer security.

Summary

Framing this another way, by familiarizing yourself with the ways in which bad actors think and how they act, you will be in a better position to understand the methods they can and will employ against targets.

With that understanding, however, you obtain not only the wisdom to protect yourself but can also wield its application with greater success toward protecting your device(s) and personal data and/or privacy.

Remember the quote earlier regarding perception and power? How one without the other serves little use? Each are intangible qualities on their own. However, when combined, the unification of these abilities are far greater than the sum of its parts when it comes to positioning you – the user or the admin – in the greatest possible situation to proactively secure your devices against future events. Savvy?

CHAPTER 5

(Return of) the Mac

Apple wasn't always the consumer's platform of choice. Through the decades, Apple has seen a fluctuation in adoption that has affected its market share. To better understand the current state of security of macOS and gain insight into where its headed, it's good to revisit Apple's history because it does play a role in combating misconceptions that linger to this very day.

For those of us that have been around long enough (i.e., since the mid-1980s), we know that the Mac never left. While this is not a summary of Apple's journey from Steve Jobs' garage to what modern day Apple looks like, 1984 was a crucial year for Apple as they marketed and sold the first consumer personal computer (PC) – the Macintosh. It was many firsts for both Apple and computing, such as sporting a graphical user interface (GUI), built-in screen and mouse, retrofitted into its all-in-one design. For home users, it was, in a word: revolutionary!

Throughout the years, several iterations of Apple computers were developed and sold to varying levels of success. Ultimately, the "misses," combined with the greater PC market's marketing of components that were licensed and thus, more affordable, led to Microsoft dominating the market share with their Windows operating system for years to come.

While this doesn't directly affect macOS security, indirectly, it plays a larger, ongoing role as you'll see. Apple's insistence on ensuring that the same Mac experience can be had by all users on all Apple hardware led to the excellent, lauded user experience we've all come to know and love. But it also came at a steep entry price, compared to generic PC components.

© Jesus Vigo, Jr. 2023
J. Vigo, Jr., *Hardening Your Macs*, https://doi.org/10.1007/978-1-4842-8939-6_5

Adding to this, the fact that developers writing software needed to rely on different codebases when authoring software, as Apple's use of proprietary hardware vs. the PC market relying on non-proprietary gear meant that code generated for PC would not work on Apple and vice versa.

Sadly, Apple continued its downward spiral, even ousting Steve Jobs along the way. Their fortunes didn't begin to turnaround until the return of Steve Jobs…and a little financial help from Bill Gates,[1] founder of Microsoft. It was only then that Apple began to turn a corner by not only creating one of the most popular computers ever – the iconic (and colorful) iMac – but has since built upon this new foundation to innovate time and again. Continuing to put incredible devices, like the iPhone and MacBook Pro into the hands of millions of users globally.

While Apple still doesn't own as much of the market share as Microsoft does, ironically its financial evaluation places Apple in the #1 spot, right above Microsoft at #2 as the most valuable technology company in the world.

To summarize, in the last four decades, Apple has been on top, tumbling down to the point of (almost) bankruptcy, then slowly built itself back up again to a company that develops, arguably, the most popular and sought-after computers and mobile devices in the world. All this growth and potential signal a healthy company…and for threat actors, it also signals a huge opportunity filled with a nearly endless supply of potential targets to compromise.

---

[1] Clifford, Catherine. "When Microsoft Saved Apple: Steve Jobs and Bill Gates Show Eliminating Competition Isn't the Only Way to Win." CNBC. CNBC, June 12, 2020. www.cnbc.com/2017/08/29/steve-jobs-and-bill-gates-what-happened-when-microsoft-saved-apple.html

macOS

The operating system that powers Mac computers has experienced a renaissance throughout the years as well.

Beginning with System Software (ver. 1.0), or System 1 in 1984, the operating system that powered Macs well into the new millennium was renamed Mac OS and now goes by the name Classic Mac OS so as not to confuse users.

Classic Mac OS 9 (formerly Mac OS 9) marked the last of the operating systems to run on Apple's PowerPC – the processor that powered its hardware up until Steve Jobs and the NeXTSTEP operating system, which was in development during his brief time away from Apple.

NeXTSTEP was later merged with the next iteration of Apple's soon-to-be released operating system – Mac OS X. The tenth in the line of OSes and based on the underpinnings of the stable, yet powerful Unix line of operating systems.

While some Apple fans lamented the change toward Mac OS X and Intel-based Mac systems (more on that later), the change would mark a historic return to form for the company as it not only drew new users to the ecosystem but growing adoption by consumers drew more developers authoring software for Apple computers. The cyclical effect continued to grow both market share and Apple's profitability.

Fast forward 15 years to 2016 and Apple has once again changed the name of its operating system, this time to macOS. But the name isn't the only notable change, as throughout the years Apple has doubled down on the user experience they're known for, as well as integration with other assorted devices, namely, the popular iPhone and iPad mobile devices. Additionally, Apple leads the industry in security and privacy (but more on that later) as they continue their path to being – and staying at – #1 as the most successful technology company in the world.

Hardware

Apple is renowned for their hardware. From the commercially designed framework adorned with solid, machined aluminum and glass on the exterior to the state-of-the-art internal components – everything that goes into the holistic design of an Apple computer draws upon the pillars or design philosophy according to Steve Jobs.

1. **Craft:** The materials used in the construction of Apple devices, the levels of, and attention to, detail present in even the most common of components and how they add to instead of taking away from the overall experience.

2. **Empathy:** Truly understanding the needs of the user. A tenet infused throughout Apple and still practiced today as evidenced by anyone that has ever had to bring their treasured device to the Genius Bar for support.

3. **Focus:** The ability to zero in on what you want to do or do better requires eliminating anything superfluous. Basically, if it doesn't help to make it better, then get rid of it.

4. **Impute:** Defined as "crediting something to a person or cause." In this case, the principle derives its meaning from designing Apple products as the best while presenting them as nothing less than the best.

5. **Friendliness:** Not pertaining to the level of approachability of its employees – although I've met many an Apple alum that are very cool people in their own right – in this case, the term relates this

feeling toward the devices Apple creates. Making technology easy to access, or friendly, invites users to enjoy using it.

6. **Simplicity:** The most obvious quality and one from which all others flow to and from is how simple Apple computers are to use, regardless of your experience level.

Put another way: Apple's **Focus** on **Simplicity** and **Craft** not only conveys the elegance and style of their computers but also **Imputes** an invitation for users to realize their potential through the **Empathy** and **Friendliness** poured into every ounce of the device – from hardware to software.

Software

Like the hardware it runs on, Apple has always been at the forefront of technology in the software realm as well. Not content to simply deliver an operating system that is both stable and secure from the ground up, Apple's adherence to the aforementioned principles of design acts as the driver in developing new, user-friendly applications, forward-thinking features that operate as natural extensions of human processes, and incorporating intuitive integrations between the hardware, software, and the way in which users get work done.

Inclusive of this is the much-vaunted Apple user experience, something that almost every Apple user, regardless of the device or experience level, can agree upon. The amount of care and innovation that goes into designing the interface for the user is second to none.

Nowhere in the software experience is attention to detail more prevalent than when considering how focused shortcuts, gestures, and the interoperability between various apps and services are with respect to user productivity. Take, for example, the Share bar. From the outside, it looks like just an entry in the context menu that allows quick sharing of a website, file, or some text with a contact or SMS recipient. But internally, the various hooks in place allow users to truly take data from one app or service and share it with another, transforming how that data can be used. All from a single click of the mouse – no launching additional applications or complex configurations to establish links between apps like we used to have to do years ago.

Distribution

In 2011, Apple released Mac OS X 10.7, also known as Lion. Apart from the new features included in the OS, the inclusion of the Mac App Store would prove to revolutionize how applications and subscription-based services would be delivered in the future.

The tried-and-true method of app deployment, by downloading applications from the developer's website and paying licensing or enrolling in a subscription plan directly with the developer is still available – even as of this writing.

But the digital delivery method introduced through the App Store has grown in popularity since its inception. So much so that the current app count hovers just north of 2 million applications and has been adopted by nearly every major Mac developer. And thanks to the model's design, it's a viable delivery stream for developers of all sizes, scaling as needed.

An additional benefit for developers and users alike is that Apple has built-in protections that actively scan software code for malware alongside other potential security threats. Furthermore, the apps are securely hosted within Apple's cloud of data centers that span the world, ensuring app availability with lightning-fast access to software for millions of macOS devices globally.

Frameworks

According to Apple's Frameworks Programming Guide,[2] *"A framework is a hierarchical directory that encapsulates shared resources, such as a dynamic shared library, nib files, image files, localized strings, header files, and reference documentation in a single package. Multiple applications can use all of these resources simultaneously."*

So, what's a framework, again? In lay terms, a framework is a collection of programming resources that are grouped together based on functionality.

The purpose of a framework is to allow developers quick access to commonly used resources, called libraries, that can be implemented into their applications to add a particular functionality, without having to redesign the group of resources that enable the functionality from scratch.

Frameworks not only enable applications to be designed with minimal resources, but since the dependencies are shared through the frameworks and the one instance of the resource is loaded into memory, apps run with minimal resources while operating at maximum efficiency.

Since this book deals with security concepts, I'd be remiss if I failed to mention two important frameworks that directly impact macOS: security[3] and privacy.[4] Additional frameworks include:

- HomeKit

- CloudKit

- SiriKit

- DriverKit

---

[2] https://developer.apple.com/library/archive/documentation/MacOSX/Conceptual/BPFrameworks/Concepts/WhatAreFrameworks.html

[3] https://developer.apple.com/documentation/security

[4] https://developer.apple.com/app-store/user-privacy-and-data-use/

- ReplayKit

- ARKit

Security

macOS is designed with security and privacy in mind. Thanks to the Unix underpinnings and increased focus on security, Apple has doubled down on the latter while implementing practices and processes that uphold end-user privacy without compromising either.

While there are a wide variety of security-enhancing features – both hardware- and software-based – that ensure this happens, an entirely separate book could be written about the internal security protections built into macOS.

This goes beyond the scope of this particular book, but we do review several common (and a few not so common) security implementations with a brief description of how they work and what the protections do to keep Mac users safe.

Without further ado, let's dive into the hardware side first.

- **Apple Silicon:** The custom designed System on a Chip (SoC) incorporates common components, such as CPU, GPU, RAM, and the Secure Enclave through security connections, allowing only verified components to perform trusted processes, through seamless integration between hardware and software.

- **T2 security chip:** Similar in design as the preceding SoC, the chip includes its own processor, RAM, and operating system (bridgeOS 2.0), including Secure Enclave. T2 secures the power on and boot sequence, including upgrading macOS and not permitting unsigned components to compromise security.

- **Secure enclave:** Located within the T2 Security chip, containing the AES Crypto Engine, Public key Accelerator, and controllers for storage, camera, microphones, ambient light sensors, and biometrics.

- **Touch ID:** The security architecture includes the biometric sensor, which captures an image of the fingerprint, but that is only one-half of the component. The other half relies on the Secure Enclave, that processes the biometric image to perform secure authentication.

Now, onto the software-based security protections of macOS:

- **Boot ROM:** The first code that executes when the system is powered on validates the Low-Level Bootstrap (LLB), then proceeds to validate the system-paired firmware.

- **Secure boot:** A series of cryptographically signed steps make up the startup process. Each step has its integrity checked before proceeding to the next. This includes the Secure Enclave, which verifies that the sepOS it uses is signed by Apple.

- **UEFI firmware security:** On Intel-based Macs, the firmware is verified by the T2 Security Chip, which contains the root of trust, helping to prevent attacks against or bypassing the UEFI firmware.

- **Signed system volume (SSV):** The system volume that has been segmented; one partition is read-only, isolating the system files, while the remaining partition stores user data.

- **FileVault:** Encryption capability that secures all data at rest with AES-XTS data encryption algorithm, utilizing the Secure Enclave's AES engine.

- **System integrity protection (SIP):** Technology that helps prevent modifying protected files and folders, such as important system directories, whether by malicious software or user error.

- **Memory protection engine:** Technology that operates in-line and independently of the Secure Enclave to encrypt data written to memory, protecting the data against attacks and preventing compromise of data through replay.

- **Gatekeeper:** Designed to ensure that only trusted software, such as that which has been code signed digitally, or Notarized, by a developer registered with Apple, runs on your Mac.

- **User data protections:** A collection of security technologies used by macOS to safeguard end-user data while upholding privacy from security threats, like malware and unauthorized access.

- **Transparency, consent, and control (TCC):** Part of the security framework that implements controls over computer's resources, like the webcam or microphone, limiting access to user data without authorization.

- **XProtect:** An antivirus tool that provides threat intelligence which quickly identifies and blocks malware detected on your Mac.

- **Malware removal tool (MRT):** A vulnerability scanner that detects and remediates against malware found on your Mac.

- **Network security:** A collection of security protocols, encryption algorithms and newer, integrated technologies that authenticate, authorize, and encrypt communications and data in transit.

- **Services security:** Security technologies that are used in Apple-created services, such as iCloud, Apple Pay, and Messages, to name a few. Each robust service is designed with user privacy and data security in mind.

- **Developer kit security:** Developer kits not only allow third-party developers to extend Apple services with new, intuitive features, but by baking in user privacy and security within each framework, it enables developers to do so securely.

- **Secure device management:** This collection of security provides flexible policies and configurations that provide an easy way to manage and enforce device security – whether as a user with a personal device that's part of a BYOD program or enterprise IT that is hardening company-owned devices.

For a full breakdown of the Apple Platform Security[5] for not only macOS, but iOS, iPadOS and tvOS, Apple maintains an updated guide via their support website that goes into granular detail over the security technologies discussed in this chapter, as well as performing a deeper

---

[5] https://support.apple.com/guide/security/secure-device-management-overview-sec38eb8731b/web

dive into the entire catalog of documented technologies that work to comprehensively protect your Apple device while safeguarding data and maintaining user privacy.

Privacy

macOS, like all other devices in the Apple ecosystem, leans heavily toward the user. After all, if Apple's history has taught us anything, it's that they design their products with the user in mind.

But more than that – Apple designs the entire experience around the user.

This translates directly into security protections that actively look after the user, maintaining their privacy and safeguarding their data while placing them in the driver's seat when it comes to managing what computer resources have access to stored data and if they're permitted to interact with that data.

Among the various security features discussed in this chapter that fortify user privacy, there are a few that we have yet to speak of and a few more that, while mentioned in the previous section, deserve further explanation.

Transparency, Consent, and Control, also referred to as TCC in short, provides users visibility into what resources are allowed to do (and denied from doing) with the data stored on the device (transparency). It provides the management interface which allows users to authorize or deny access to resources, data, and applications (consent). Finally, it acts as the central system by which user-based settings are enforced across the entire system, upholding the user's privacy, based on their desired level of threat tolerance (control).

For example, you install a collaboration app, like the ones used to participate in virtual meetings. Upon first launch, it will prompt you to authorize or deny access to the webcam and microphone. It may also ask to allow the app to access your contacts and Desktop folder.

Considering that virtual meetings often rely on the camera and microphone for participants to communicate, it makes sense to allow the app access to these resources. Requesting access to your contacts could be seen as invasive, but again, if you think about it, the ability to access contact data in order to send invites for scheduled meetings actually saves users time, so that request may make sense too.

However, why does a collaboration app that allows users to participate in virtual meetings in real-time need access to read and write to your Desktop folder? Unless you're sharing or saving documents from/to that specific location, it may be best to deny that part of the request to preserve your privacy, but keep all data stored in that directory safe.

Mic indicator, found in the Control Center within the Menu bar is another example of those "user first" design principles Apple bakes into macOS. When an application accesses the microphone on your Mac, a small orange dot appears in the top-right corner of the Control Center, indicating the mic was used. Clicking on it will reveal the name of the app that used it last.

iCloud offers several privacy features that offer protections for email and Internet access, respectively. While part of the iCloud+ subscription service offering, each of the following features is available on Macs running at least macOS Monterey.

- **Mail privacy protection:** Working with the Apple Mail app prevents senders from obtaining identifiable information about you, the recipient, such as when you view messages, how many times it was viewed, if it was forwarded, or the IP address of the device you viewed it from.

- **Hide my email:** This feature allows users to create unique and randomized email address aliases to use when sending and receiving email messages. This way, your real email address is always hidden from potential threat actors looking to send you spam or leverage the address for a future attack, such as spoofing.

- **iCloud private relay:** While the previous entries dealt with email privacy, this one pertains to keeping your Internet activity private. When enabled, web requests are sent through two separate yet secure relays. The first relay is operated by Apple and encrypts your request, yet allows them to see your real IP address. The encrypted request is sent to a third-party provider where they retrieve the requested content and generate a temporary IP address, connecting you to the website requested. Neither relay can see your DNS records, as they are encrypted to keep your browsing history private – even from Apple. Additionally, a setting for IP Address Location exists, which allows users to specify if you prefer a more localized temporary IP address or a generalized IP address (one that is generated within the country and time zone you're physically located in).

Summary

With the plethora of hardware and software protections built-in to macOS and your Mac computer, users are armed with considerable technology tools to strengthen security and protect their privacy from many threats in the wild.

Becoming familiar with these tools is only half the battle, the other half lies in not only enabling these settings to actively safeguard your data and privacy but also in periodically checking them to make sure that no unauthorized access has inadvertently been granted – whether by you, a malicious user with access to your device, or some potentially unwanted application or malware that changed it without your consent.

In addition to the preceding, let's not forget common sense. This is not a dig against you or your users, but rather a "wake up" call letting you know that despite the growing number of Apple-focused threats out in the wild, there's a significant number of them that can simply be protected against by simply applying logic to think through what is being requested.

Remember the example provided earlier about the collaboration software? The first two requests made sense since that is precisely what this type of app is used for; the third request may or may not apply to you specifically, so tread carefully; however, the fourth request clearly did not fit in with the other requests and stuck out like a sore thumb. Approving it, despite the warning signs, is not the correct call for preserving data security or user privacy.

With all things security- or privacy-related, consider the adage, "*if it's too good to be true, it probably is.*"

PART II

Welcome to the Rock

The first several chapters of this book concern themselves with background information, defining terms and explaining the various security technologies that are native to macOS. Such is the blend of hardware and software, algorithms and frameworks, that are built-in to each Mac, whose sole focus is to work in harmony toward the protection of your Apple computer, keeping sensitive data secured and preserving user privacy from modern and evolving threats. In Part II of this book, we go further down the security path by grouping the following three chapters that focus exclusively on the techniques, settings, and configurations that heighten internal and external security protections to holistically secure your Mac.

CHAPTER 6

Lock It Down

What is meant by the reference, "locking down your computer"?

Viewed through the lens of security, it refers to a series of processes and practices that serve to ultimately restrict the open settings on your Mac by configuring them in such a way as to change their default state, which is not only commonly known but such knowledge makes your computer easier to attack.

Put another way: locking down your computer means changing the device settings from their defaults to a more secured state.

It and the term "hardening" are both terms I will use throughout this chapter (and likely the remainder of the book) – both of which – alongside "minimizing the attack surface" are all mutually exclusive and refer to the same process.

Other terms that are used frequently in computer security are "vectors" and "workarounds." Both of which have very different meanings from each other, as well as different meanings to the preceding hardening, but we'll get into their meanings later in this chapter.

Hardening Process

The term hardening, as discussed in the previous section, refers to a series of practices, processes, steps, and workflows that are taken to strengthen the overall hardware and software security of your Mac. The steps taken are grounded in best practices and often aligned with a security framework.

© Jesus Vigo, Jr. 2023
J. Vigo, Jr., *Hardening Your Macs*, https://doi.org/10.1007/978-1-4842-8939-6_6

But let's not get too ahead of ourselves, we go into greater depth in Chapter 10 about security frameworks and what benefits they provide when aligning your security practices with one or more of them.

For the purposes of this chapter, let's focus on how hardening works, why it's important, and how to start locking down your own device or the ones you're responsible for to maximize security protections.

Hardening can apply to both software (macOS) and hardware (Mac computer) and should be applied to both as part of a comprehensive security plan. But before we get bogged down with how to identify what settings need reinforcement, consider that settings are largely just a grouping of preferences. This might make it easier to target certain areas and not make the process seem so daunting.

For example, one of the most common settings that most users implement from the moment they power on their Mac for the first time is setting a password. By default, macOS does not have a password preselected for you, instead it prompts you to create one during the initial setup process. Should you choose to not select a password, that's your prerogative and your device (and personal data) will be accessible to anyone with physical access to your Mac.

As with most security-based processes, the way in which certain settings are configured will have a noticeable, sometimes direct, impact on other security settings and their efficacy. Take, for example, the previous no password scenario. Not enabling a password also means that FileVault encryption cannot be enabled as the service relies on the user's password to serve as the key that unlocks the storage disk, thereby decrypting the data.

No password equals no encryption. No encryption equals no protection from unauthorized access or modification of your data, should your Mac become lost, stolen, or otherwise fall into the hands of someone else, even temporarily.

While your specific tolerance for data loss may be different from everyone else, you should ask yourself: If I lost my computer right this minute, how would I feel if my data was exposed to the public? Think of the memories captured within photos, connections made and maintained through social media accounts, critical work documents, including chat logs and email threads or even highly sensitive records pertaining to financial transactions.

This is not accounting for the loss of data and your ability to regain access to it, but merely the concept of that very data being made available for anyone to see in an instant. Sadly, for many of us, this has long-standing ripple effects, not unlike dropping a stone into a pristine lake…eventually, the smallest ripples grow outward into larger and larger imprints on the water's surface.

In a nutshell, hardening your device is incredibly important. The reasons why you need to protect your data are vast and span far beyond just exposure of data. Some of these relate to identity theft or impersonation of your character to gain access to your family and friends. Also, many of these crimes are financially motivated since there is a lot of money to be made by bad actors stealing your Personally Identifiable Information (PII) and selling it on the dark web. Lastly, this applies more to businesses, but accessing confidential data is a significant concern, both from a liability perspective for the company and impacting the on-going operation of the company. Say, for example, there are classified prototype plans for a new version of a product your company is working on. Should these plans be stolen and made public knowledge, the organization could end up going out of business due to the loss of investment in the technology. If not, the potential loss of revenue could also be a cause that dooms the organization in the future.

Minimizing the Attack Surface

Every device, regardless of who designed it or on what OS it runs, has an attack surface. This relates directly to the area of the device that may be susceptible to attack, including both hardware and software resources.

Every device and operating system is different. There's no "one size fits all" or "just right" amount of attack surface. The goal should always be to limit it as much as possible or tolerable.

To put it into perspective, picture a large, open field. Acres upon acres of land and cattle grazing. Got the visual, yet? Ok, good. So, this vast plain represents your Mac's attack surface and the cattle represents the software resources, like files, PII, and other sensitive data types. Managing such a large field could prove difficult for just one person, a lone rancher (the rancher in this example represents you, the user).

Threats to consider to your field and cattle are wild animals, like hyenas that can attack your cattle, natural occurrences, like tornados can also impact your field and cattle. Lastly, fires and insects can severely hurt both as well. But the logistics of managing all those threats are near impossible as is. The solution is to reconfigure the ranch so that it offers greater protection against the varied threats.

For example, you fence in an area and build a barn to contain your cattle but mitigate against the hyena and tornado threats. You can install irrigation systems throughout the parts of the land susceptible to fire, while provisioning fumigation systems to protect those sections of the land that are prone to insects.

You're not eliminating land size, but rather you're subdividing it in such a way so that it addresses your needs while minimizing the concerns. Well, that is much the same as the guiding principle behind minimizing the attack surface: You work with what you have to limit the potentiality for threats by reconfiguring how that feature, function, or resource works. In strengthening it, you are also strengthening the overall security of your Mac.

Put another way, consider an office building with one front and side entrance, along with not one but two rear entrances. At any given time, there are four potential doorways to enter and leave the property. From a physical security viewpoint, this represents a bit of a nightmare since you may not have adequate personnel to cover each ingress and egress properly against trespassers.

So, the next best solution is to whittle the potential four entrances down to two. The front entrance is for incoming visitors, with adequate security controls to ensure that each visitor is tapping their ID to gain access. No ID? Security guards are physically monitoring each user, ensuring that those without access are not allowed in. The two rear entrances now are converted into an exit where outgoing visitors are funneled out the doors and onto the parking lot with physical security staff present to ensure no one doubles-back in from the one-way doors. The side entrance is kept locked and secured with cameras and rotating security staff making sure no one enters or exits through here.

It's still the same building, with the same number of visitors and grounds that security staff must cover. But the vectors, which we'll get into in the next section, are identified and have been secured to prevent unauthorized access except from the designated front entrance and rear exit.

Identifying Vectors

Vectors play a significant role in shrinking the attack surface of your Mac system. See, vectors are the name given to the points in which an attack may be possible. It could and certainly will be multiple vectors that impact your Mac. The variance of vectors will depend on you. Specifically, how tolerable the risk may (or may not) be, which in turn scales the vector higher or lower on the scale of priority.

Don't get the message confused though. While the risk assessment process discussed in Chapter 2 lends itself to a lot of leeway based on what you – the user – determine as A) risk; and B) the criticality of identified risk; just as not all risk is created equal, neither are all vectors.

Some vectors are known in the security community to be far more critical than others – regardless of your personal feelings on the matter. This is not to be rude but rather to underscore that something as trivial or irksome as having to enter a password each time you use your computer is very much considered a big deal. Remember the analogy about the stone causing larger ripple effects in the lake? Well, some vectors which seem like the smallest of stones create the largest of ripple effects, so it's best to approach each objectively.

Still, some vectors may simply not apply to you and your specific use case. This doesn't mean it's not important or even a good idea to protect against it, but it may not be high on your list of things to watch out for, with others more pertinent deserving a larger share of the spotlight.

Consider disk encryption. For anyone with a mobile device, like a MacBook Pro or Air, it makes a lot more sense to enable encryption due to its mobile nature. This doesn't mean that your iMac doesn't need an encrypted storage drive because lugging around a 20+ lbs. computer seems counter-intuitive. Encryption is still an important, critical security control, often considered "the last barrier" to keeping data safe from unauthorized access.

But it does mean that just as you should always assess risk as it pertains to your unique needs while balancing it with best practices, so too should vectors be considered in a similar light.

Another way to consider vectors is to ask the question, how do I access or perform X function? The "X" in this case is a variable representing multiple values. If you ask, how do I login to my computer? And the answer is, without a password. Then that answer can apply to anyone that comes in contact with your computer – not just you. However, if you answered, "with a password," because you set a password, then a logical follow-up question is, "who knows my password?"

This line of questioning continues on, further fleshing out the details of how critical the vector is while simultaneously identifying the proposed solution to mitigating against the vector.

I use the word mitigating here and not resolving because, depending on the vector itself, there could be a solution that resolves the problem outright as is the case many times. Sometimes however, there is no real or permanent solution available, which leads directly to what we'll be discussing in the next section.

Workarounds

What is a workaround? you may be thinking. It is a temporary action taken to "fix" an issue. Please note that I use the word *fix* here loosely since workarounds themselves are not fully functioning solutions to issues nor do they resolve vectors themselves. They merely act as place holders to minimize exposure from vectors and threats until a proper solution has been developed and implemented.

I know this sounds like semantics or play on words, but it is a very real thing that occurs all the time in computer security, just as in life.

Example time. I recently came home to find my water heater sprang a leak from the hot water valve, causing quite the steamy mess. The valve developed a kink over time and eventually the kink became a perforation from where the water leaked out, effectively soaking half of the items in my pantry. As Murphy's would have it, no plumbers were available until the following morning and despite turning off the heater's water valve, water was still shooting out. So I grabbed a replacement valve I had and fashioned that on to temporarily fix (ok, it made less water leak out) the issue until morning when a plumber was able to assess that the root cause of the problem came from the water heater gone bad, facilitating a replacement.

The solution in this scenario was replacing the water heater unit completely. But the workaround (temporary fix) was to replace the valve from where the majority of the water had been leaking from, while additionally shutting the water valve off.

I could have shut off the main water valve completely and that would've "resolved the problem" to an extent. But I'm partial to my hot showers and keeping the main water valve closed would have cut all the water flowing into my home, so that's not really a good solution moving forward, is it?

And that's the point of workarounds, they're tantamount to band aids. Good for a temporary, small-time fix until a long-term solution becomes available. Sometimes, they're all you have. Some security vulnerabilities discovered are so deep-rooted that the fix will take the developers some time to properly investigate, test, and deploy. A great recent example of using a workaround until a fully fleshed out solution is available was the relatively recent Log4j vulnerability.[1] Pronounced "*log forge*," it affected software applications that relied on Java libraries, targeting how data was written to logs and allowing attackers to forge entries at will on affected systems.

While the vulnerability has long been fixed, with relevant patches provided by affected developers for their respective applications, the initial reports of the vulnerability were followed almost immediately by bad actors attempting to exploit it in the wild. With such global implications stemming from Java libraries being used in any number of use cases, a

---

[1] www.jamf.com/blog/protect-your-organization-against-log4j-java-based-exploit/

solution was not immediately available. Instead, app developers were providing their clients and users guidance on how their product was specifically affected and often included several workarounds that allowed companies to continue using the product while limiting the potential for exposure to attack.

In this and many other cases, workarounds were used temporarily in lieu of a permanent solution, which became available shortly thereafter. The point of workarounds isn't to resolve the problem once and for all, but act as a stop-gap measure that limits exposure to the threat *until* the actual solution is made available.

There are scenarios of course where users employ workarounds in place of solutions, believing that the root cause is resolved and fixing the problem. This is an error and great care should be taken to prevent situations like this from occurring, since workarounds tend to focus on just getting the feature or function to continue to work as intended without really fixing the root or central cause of the problem in the first place. This means that, if left unchecked, workarounds used as long-term solutions provide a false sense of security at best while still leaving the core problem unresolved, which is exactly what a threat actor needs to exploit the issue and compromise your system and data.

One last note about workarounds, reiterating the preceding, they are not meant as a permanent solution. Sometimes, I would encounter organizations deploying workarounds to hardware or software issues because a solution did not exist. Not just at the moment, but like one was never going to exist due to a series of complicated circumstances. While it's not too common, it still does happen, and it is usually attributed to a "perfect storm" of issues stemming from outdated or obsolete hardware and combining with software bugs that require extensive solutions to resolve completely.

One example I can think of related to a piece of software that relied on a HASP, which is a hardware tool, like a specially modified USB drive that contained proprietary data on it that would verify the license of the software, permitting it to operate properly. The issue stemmed from the HASP and how it interfaced with computer hardware created before a certain time and a specific operating system. The HASP would work just fine on older hardware and OS, but if a certain required update was applied to the OS, the HASP would fail to load. The developer worked with the hardware and OS vendor, and ultimately, the solution was to continue using the older OS without the critical update or update to the latest version of the software which also required the latest version of the OS, resulting in doubled expenses for the organization for the latter solution or minimized security with the former solution.

Summary

With this chapter, we learned about the hardening process:

- What it is

- What it does

- Why it's important

We also covered the attack surface and what it means to minimize it, further reducing the attack surface provides greater management over hardware and software resources, tying directly into maintaining a strong device security posture.

Diving deeper into the hardening process, the topic of vectors was touched upon. Specifically, explaining how vectors are like open doors to your Mac, giving threat actors the opening they need to attack your system in any number of ways. Additionally, how to identify vectors – through independent assessment or by aligning your organization's security practices with known security frameworks – to provide guidance on how to mitigate risk to security threats specific to your needs or that of your organization.

Last but most definitely not least: workarounds. The temporary fixes to identified threats by vectors that comprise processes that, while not a fully baked solution that resolves the underlying problem, offer users a means to mitigate risk – at least in part – while allowing continued use of the feature, function, or resource, until the developer has ample time to research, develop, test, and deploy a true solution to permanently resolve the core issue, threat, or vulnerability.

CHAPTER 7

The Outer Limits

Securing your Mac occurs when you harden or lock down various settings within your Apple computer. These settings, as mentioned previously, fall into two separate categories that – when combined – make up a comprehensive security plan to keep Mac protected.

The first of these categories is external security protections and the various settings that make up this section will be discussed here in great depth, alongside step-by-step instructions (when allowable) to configure these settings for maximum security against threats that are known to target and affect all external vectors that exist within your Apple computer.

Startup

A system's startup, in this context, doesn't refer to powering on your computer, but rather the underlying software that controls the basic functionality of the hardware within a computer.

In Macs that are designed with Intel processors, it is known as the Unified Extensible Firmware Interface (UEFI), or sometimes shortened to EFI. For newer Macs running Apple Silicon like the M-series processors, the boot process is part of the Secure Enclave and despite a few differences, provides largely the same functionality as UEFI. This code also goes by the more universally accepted name: firmware is found in just about every piece of technology – from optical disc players to navigation systems to, of course, your Apple computer. It is low-level code that is

© Jesus Vigo, Jr. 2023
J. Vigo, Jr., *Hardening Your Macs*, https://doi.org/10.1007/978-1-4842-8939-6_7

responsible for basic functions, like telling the system how it should handle button presses, such as when you press the power button to power on your Mac, for example.

It also contains code that handles the way components and subcomponents perform tasks. One example of this is seen when you boot your Mac. Typically, the Mac will power on and initiate the boot process, being told by firmware to find the relevant boot files for macOS within the Startup Disk. This process occurs the same way each time by default.

However, Intel-based Macs do provide users the option to boot to other sources, by simply holding down the Option key while powering on your device. This keyboard combination will invoke the boot menu to be displayed to the user instead of booting directly to the default disk. Users and administrators may wish to use this when booting to a different disk, maybe one included via USB storage or perhaps to boot from optical media if your computer has an optical storage device attached or when running diagnostics on your Mac.

While the reasons for doing so may vary, the end result is the same: the user may need to boot to an alternative disk at times and this is the way to accomplish this task. Simple enough, yet it also poses a significant security risk if not secured, since it allows virtually anyone with physical access to your computer to boot to a potentially unauthorized environment where full access to your data could provide an attacker the opportunity to read, modify, copy, or delete data without restrictions.

It could also allow bad actors to change certain settings within your Mac, such as modifying system files, planting malware, removing security protections and/or creating or modifying user accounts and their access permissions – some without leaving a trace that your system and/or data's integrity has been compromised – such as resetting your account's password.

While the attacks surrounding Startup can vary, luckily enough, preventing attacks comes down to just one, simple task that must be performed once to effectively lock down and protect users against these threats.

Setting a Startup password (Intel-based Mac):

1. Boot to macOS Recovery mode by pressing and holding the Command and R keys while powering on your Mac.

2. From the macOS Recovery window, click on Utilities ➤ Startup Security Utility, or Firmware Password Utility.

3. Next, a new window will open. Click on the Turn On Firmware... Password button.

4. Enter a password in the New password field and the Verify field, then click on the Set Password button to save your changes.

5. Last, click on the Apple menu | Reset to reboot your Mac.

Note For setting a firmware password on Apple Silicon-based Macs, see the process to enable volume-level encryption in the next section as Apple has tied both functionalities to each other.

That's it! The password has been set and will be required when attempting to change the boot process or simply boot to a device besides the default disk where macOS is installed. This also includes protections against booting to macOS Recovery locally or over the Internet, Safe Mode, or Apple Diagnostics.

It should go without saying (but I'll say it anyway for good measure), remember this password! Without it, you won't be able to make additional changes to the underlying system. As a safety precaution, Apple has designed this function so that in the event that your device is lost, stolen or simply accessed by an unauthorized user, changes cannot be made without the password.

The bad news is that should you forget the firmware password, an appointment for service with Apple will be required in order to reset a forgotten password after providing proof of ownership, of course.

Volume-Level Encryption

Apple's implementation of volume-level encryption is called FileVault. You'll find this appears both in this chapter for external protection, as well as the next chapter for internal protections. This is because I've split them with the purpose of identifying the reasons to enable this feature for external reasons here, while steering the discussion toward internal benefits in the next chapter. Another reason for this split is that Apple computers that contain the T2 chip or Secure Enclave already benefit from volume-level encryption that occurs automatically on-the-fly and is decrypted when the login prompt is displayed.

It may seem redundant, excessive, or even unnecessary to enable FileVault if you have a T2 or Secure Enclave-enabled Mac. Since those devices already offer volume-level encryption by default, the former is no longer required for data security, right? Yes and no.

Yes, because volume-level encryption means data is encrypted and this prevents access to the data on the disk while it's powered on. At the same time, the answer is No because it requires the device to be operating within macOS. If the storage device were to be removed from your Mac, like the way some SSDs are, the key stored within T2 or the Secure Enclave would not be able to encrypt the data, therefore leaving it decrypted.

But what if the SSD is soldered to the logic board and cannot be removed, then it's safe? You might think so, but there's still the possibility that the Mac could be booted into Target Disk Mode, which does not boot macOS, instead leaving the Mac to operate as an external drive (source) that can be connected to another Mac (destination) over a Thunderbolt cable. Since macOS does not boot in this mode, the data on the source remains decrypted and accessible to the destination Mac. From there, an attacker will be able to view the directories on the source Mac without worry of encryption, just as if they were scrolling through the file system natively. In this case, FileVault is the only technology that would effectively stop an attacker in their tracks, requiring them to know the credentials to a FileVault-approved account or the recovery key to successfully unlock the volume.

With regards to external security, volume-level encryption is an absolute must for anyone that is mobile or always on the go. After all, the more you travel with your Mac, the more likely you are to be affected by risk from loss or theft. While encryption doesn't provide mitigation against losing your Mac or it being stolen, it does offer protection of your data against those that wish to access sensitive or critical data without authorization to do so and selling it off to the highest bidder.

While encryption has long been viewed as an essential technology for mobile users, due to wide adoption of other Apple devices, such as iPhone and iPad – combined with growing adoption of more holistic security technologies – encrypting your Mac with FileVault is not only incredibly effective at mitigating risk to your data, but the encryption level used by Mac is quite strong. Plus, the process to enable the feature for end-user's is as simple as toggling on a setting (more on how to enable this in the next chapter).

For now, let's focus instead on the specifics of how Apple's implementation of volume-level encryption works, beginning with what makes the type of encryption used in FileVault.

First, I've used the phrase "volume level" to refer to the type of encryption and you may be thinking, are there other types? Yes, there are. There are file-based encryption methods that protect just a particular file, such as password protecting a PDF or ZIP file. FileVault offers encryption that scrambles all the data on the disk – not just your personal files. This includes system files, swap disks (which act as temporary memory) and files created dynamically, such as when you put your Mac to sleep, to maintain the current state.

FileVault as designed by Apple protects all data stored on disk from being viewed by unauthorized users. In this case, unauthorized users are classified by the system as anyone that does not have a password to unlock the data *and* said password must be linked to an account that has been granted access by an administrator to have secure login permissions. Without authorization – even if you have a local account on the Mac or attempt to connect to the encrypted drive – all the data will remain scrambled until an authorized password is entered.

So how does encryption work to ensure your data stays safe?

Let's break it down with a quick cryptography lesson. Encryption, like the method used in FileVault, uses algorithms (also called ciphers) to mathematically compute how a particular encryption method will work. Thinking of it as a guide, it helps take data and develop the possible combinations to scramble the data, so it is unreadable by anyone without the key.

Keys, much like their physical nature, provide a means of unlocking or – in the case of cryptography – unscrambling data.

In the case of FileVault, Apple specifically uses the XTS-AES algorithm in block-cipher chain mode, using 128-bit blocks and a 256-bit key. The block-cipher chain mode portion refers to data being encrypted in whole blocks of 128-bits each. The 256-bit key is used to encrypt the entire disk.

Cable Lock

Apple manufactures its Mac computers with industrial design principles in mind. Sleek and stylish, yet intuitive and packed with the latest technology – a careful blend of form, function, and power. This makes for a modern, sophisticated computing tool for not only you – the user – but for anyone that wishes to take advantage of the advanced tech packed into Mac...even if it means taking yours.

This isn't intended to point fingers or take a negative view of society, but rather to say that there's nothing wrong with being prepared. After all, that's what security is about at its core – protecting yourself, your computer, and your data by being as ready as possible against potential threats.

Unfortunately, being ready means having to look at the possible negatives (also see risk assessment) in order to have a clearer understanding of how to best mitigate against risk. For users that are mobile, choosing to perform their computing tasks on the go means loss or theft of your computer is a very real concern.

Despite many places being set up to facilitate remote work, such as coffee shops, bookstores, and other locales open to the public, offering comfortable seating, Wi-Fi hotspots or even larger areas perfect for collaboration and conferencing foster the remote work ethos while serving as an area ripe with targets for theft of equipment.

It may not seem feasible to set up your work area then dismantle it each time you need to step away to use the restroom, take a private call or simply refill your cup o' tea. Hence why cable locks exist for every manner of Apple device, providing a strong locking mechanism attached to a cable that tethers your Mac to a table or other solid, foundational surface which makes stealing your Mac device that much more difficult.

Sensor Covers

The aim of this chapter is protecting your Mac from external threats that would otherwise impact you, your work, and how you work. While not exactly a security issue per se, there are all manner of dust and debris that can find its way inside the open ports on your Mac, such as USB and headphone jacks, that users rely on daily to get work done.

Whether it's transferring data to and from your Mac or plugging in headphones to privately participate in virtual meetings – you never really realize how much reliance is placed on these ports until they are jammed or break due to something getting in there that perhaps shouldn't have.

For times like this, sensor or port covers made of rubber or silicone are highly recommended. By affixing these little grommets into their respective ports, it keeps the ports on your computer free from dirt, dust, debris, and liquids that would otherwise find their way into your device, potentially causing more damage to your computer than just shorting out the port.

These are often inexpensive and may even be included as part of a bundle that includes other protective accessories that work to keep your devices operating more smoothly through preventative maintenance, which minimizes wear and tear in the long run.

Accessories

Similar to the sensor covers discussed in the previous section, this section will discuss the use of accessories on and in your Mac and the possible security ramifications they might present to you and your Mac.

While it's virtually impossible to cover each and every accessory created for Apple computers and how they vary based on model, this section will stick to a few of the more commonly used accessories and why they are a good (or maybe not so good) idea as it relates to cybersecurity.

- **Privacy screens**: Screen protectors are great to protect your monitor's screen from minor hazards, like chips and scratches. But these do little for security. However, those infused with privacy technology, such as tinted protectors that filter out viewing angles to prevent shoulder surfing, or someone casually looking over your shoulder as you type your password or work with sensitive data, are great to minimize the risk of those types of attack.

- **Docking stations**: Another excellent addition to add functionality to your Mac and maximize your productivity potential. Be mindful to not leave these unattended, as anyone can slip in a USB drive or microSD card with malicious code that can be used to compromise your device or simply copy your data without your knowledge.

- **External storage devices**: USB flash drives and external hard drives are great for keeping data backed up, but just like your Mac, the more mobility the greater the risk of loss or theft. Fortunately, just like your Mac, these devices should be encrypted to keep data safe from prying eyes.

- **Input devices**: Mice and keyboards are perfect examples of devices used while working with computers to get work accomplished. While they may seem innocuous enough, there are known cases of these types of devices being modified to spy on and record user data, like keystrokes.

- **Cases**: Plastic cases serve to protect the look and finish of your Mac from scratches. Though they tend to do little to fortify security, they do an admirable job of keeping them safe against the usual damage from drops or liquid spills.

- **Wireless devices**: It's difficult to get anything done without Internet access it seems, but that's all the more reason to remain vigilant when connecting to wireless networks and connecting to devices through Bluetooth. Bad actors know these connections are usually powered on and broadcasting, meaning it's easier to try and connect to your device for any manner of attack. If possible, both are best to disable when not in use.

- **Webcam covers**: With remote work thriving over meetings driven through webcam interaction, it's likely that users tend to rely on it throughout much of their day. What about when you're not using it? Recent malware targeted macOS has been designed to grab personnel data, such as recording users without their consent through their webcam. Webcam covers can mitigate unauthorized recordings by providing a mechanism to block the camera's view when it's not supposed to be in use.

- **Smart card readers**: While smart cards are a commonly used security control, they aren't used in many companies. However, if yours does or simply you want to implement smart card technology[1] for yourself, there are readers (and USB tokens) that connect to your Mac to authenticate the user, further adding to access protections.

One accessory type omitted on purpose from this section are cables and, by extension, adapters. These deserve their own section and will be covered in the next section.

---

[1] https://support.apple.com/guide/deployment/use-a-smart-card-depc705651a9/web

Licensed Cables

For the final section in this chapter about protections to external security, this portion is devoted to cables and AC adapters used to connect peripherals to your Mac.

Why cordon off cabling into their own section instead of keeping them along with the other accessories, you ask? That's a good question! They were kept deliberately apart because cables are used for everything from connecting devices to Mac to delivering resources, such as power. And while this seems straightforward enough as it does with computers from other manufacturers, Apple uses some cables that utilize proprietary technology which they license (for a fee) to manufacturers that wish to implement said technology in their cables.

What exactly this technology does depends on the cable, but the driving reason behind all the variety of cables is the same: it has to do with providing the maximum level of performance and security between your Mac and the peripheral itself.

Security plays a huge role in this because the use of licensed products ensures users that the item, a cable in this case, meets or exceeds Apple's stringent requirements. In relation to security, counterfeit or unlicensed cables will often use lower quality materials which have led to fire hazards or even damaging the Mac its connected to on one end of the spectrum; on the other end, bad actors have modified unlicensed cables to include keyloggers or malware delivery payloads that actually work to attack and compromise your system, exploiting the implicit trust users have that the cable is just a cable and won't try to actively steal their data.

Have you ever connected an iPhone to your Mac and received a request from your Mac/iPhone to authorize connecting the devices by selecting Trust or Don't Trust? In this case, that's to protect the data stored on the iPhone from being transferred to another device without permission.

But you don't receive prompts like that when connecting a keyboard, USB Flash Drive or even an AC adapter to charge your Mac, do you? You don't. At least, not yet.[2]

This is due to the underlying software not having caught up to modern security concerns just yet, but Apple is getting there. Even when it does introduce this security measure, it's still an excellent practice to rely only on licensed cables and AC adapters for the security and protection of your Mac.

This guidance goes hand in hand with the best practice of never plugging in a USB drive from an unknown source or borrowing a cable from someone you're not familiar with. Cables that have been doctored to include technology to bypass built-in security mechanisms on your Mac may not be mass produced, easy to come by, or even inexpensive – as going the DIY route could cost around two hundred dollars to manufacture.

But that's not the point really, what is important to note is that the technology is available in the wild and therefore possible, the only thing necessary to pull off this attack is a little motivation.

Summary

In this chapter, we discussed the theory behind protection of external vectors and the potential risk they present for threats to succeed.

We also went hands-on, where possible, providing step-by-step instructions on how to configure your Mac computer to safeguard it and private data against external threats.

Where instructions were not feasible or unnecessary, guidance was provided regarding:

---

[2] https://9to5mac.com/2022/06/06/macos-ventura-usb-security/

- What threats target external vectors.

- How these threats and attacks work.

- What users can do to protect themselves.

Additionally, in certain cases, we covered ways to avoid or minimize the risk associated with certain threats, also discussing some steps and considerations to take when using certain hardware peripherals and technologies alongside your Mac to further minimize risk and exposure.

CHAPTER 8

Inside Job

We continue down the path to hardening the settings within your Apple computer – this time we change gears slightly to focus on the internal, or software, side of your Mac.

Similar to the previous chapter, we discuss the various technological and feature settings that make up this section in great depth, including step-by-step instructions (where allowable) to configure these settings for maximum security. Doing so can prevent threats that are known to target and affect all internal vectors that exist within your Apple computer, seeking to compromise Mac, steal your data and even invade your privacy, using the built-in resources to spy on your every move – when you least expect it!

Passwords

We've **all** heard the warnings:

- Use a strong password

- Make sure they're all unique

- Keep them to a minimum of 12 characters

- Use multiple key spaces, mixing upper- and lower-case letters, numbers and symbols

- It should be easy for you to remember but hard for others to guess

© Jesus Vigo, Jr. 2023
J. Vigo, Jr., *Hardening Your Macs*, https://doi.org/10.1007/978-1-4842-8939-6_8

- Don't write it down anywhere

- Like your toothbrush, don't share it

- Change it every three months

- Never reuse a password you've already used

- Don't let your browser(s) remember your passwords for you

And despite these ominous warnings we've been hearing for decades…here we are, still talking about password safety. It's not because this book is short on topics to cover mind you. Passwords are still problematic for many users to manage effectively yet so easy to give up the crown jewels when a bad actor relies on exploiting the victim's "humanness" through phishing campaigns over email, social media, and SMS/text messaging.

That's one of the dominant reasons behind why phishing attacks are still the number one form of attack against users. It's because it's so darn successful at gaining user credentials with little to no effort on behalf of the attacker.

Little risk meets great reward.

While this chapter focuses on internal protections, it is important to bear in mind various threats that target protections and how some solutions are better fit to mitigate against threats than others.

In the case of passwords, how strong or difficult-to-guess your chosen password isn't particularly effective against phishing attempts if the user is merely sharing their password, but we'll discuss effective mitigation strategies against phishing later in this chapter.

For now, let's keep the focus on passwords, how to make them as strong and hard to guess as possible, while safeguarding them from threat actors and, well, ourselves. Let's start by revisiting the preceding suggestions and making a few modifications to them to protect against the modern threat landscape, shall we?

- Always use a strong password comprising multiple key spaces and at a minimum of 20 characters.

- All passwords must be unique, never duplicating or reusing prior credentials.

- Change your passwords every 45–60 days for critical accounts/services; 90–180 days for less critical accounts/services.

- Never write passwords down, store them on sticky notes anywhere near your computers, or allow the browser to remember them for you – in short, never share your password.

- If you insist on creating your own passwords, base them on something familiar to you but not something others can easily guess. For example, if your first-grade teacher's name is "Smith" transform it into something like: "/\/\iZz$m1+H_gR@d30nE."

- Better yet, eliminate the potential to reuse passwords and utilize password management software and set it to create unique passwords of a minimum length and strength every time.

If you're an administrator, the addition of password policies to this list sets requirements on how end users create passwords while implementing enforcement of compliance, requiring users to change passwords at predetermined intervals and further restricting the reuse of previous passwords.

It really **cannot** be stressed enough just how useful and important to the overall password security strategy password managers are for end users. When used properly, securely, and integrated into macOS – operating as a natural extension of the user experience – the balance of password security and meeting (often exceeding) organizational requirements simply makes the entire management process a breeze while keeping users secured.

And the best part? Apple already integrates a strong password generator and management tool into macOS with Keychain Access! Better still? Apple developed Keychain into iCloud, offering users a native, secure password management tool that takes the headache out of securing and managing your passwords. Additionally, it safeguards them against unauthorized access with your iCloud credentials while offering further protection through Two-Factor Authentication (2FA) and biometric security via Touch or Face ID technologies.

But that's not all, it leverages the cloud to encrypt and synchronize your stored credentials across all your Apple devices so passwords are up-to-date and easily accessible from any macOS or iOS-based device you sign-in to. Oh, and it's free to all Apple users, so there's really no reason to not have greater password security for all your accounts.

Manually set up a new secure password using Keychain Access

1. Navigate to Applications | Utilities | Keychain Access.app

2. Double-click it to launch it.

3. Open opening, select the "*Local Items*" keychain under the **Default Keychains** section in the navigation bar to the left.

4. From the menu bar, click File | New Password Item...

5. A new window will open. Provide a name for the new entry under the **Keychain Item Name** section.

6. Next, enter the username and password in the **Account Name** and **Password** fields, respectively.

7. If you wish to have the system auto generate a strong password for you, clicking the key icon next to the password field will bring up the Password Assistant menu. From here, you can generate a random, yet strong, password based on criteria, such as key space and length.

8. Once the data has been entered, click the "Add" button to save the record.

The preceding instructions are for manually creating entries. However, since this software is native to macOS, when visiting websites in Safari or entering credentials in Apple's first-party apps and services, macOS will automatically prompt the user if they wish to save this data to Keychain. By agreeing, a new record will be created.

If you wish to manage or simply review the list of saved passwords and which accounts are linked, navigating to **System Preferences | Passwords** allows authorized users to view this information *after* they've authenticated using their login account password or biometrics, if that feature is enabled.

For those that are not fans of putting all your eggs in one basket, can't use iCloud's services, or wish to have greater control over their sensitive password data, there are several excellent, third-party solutions available that do just as good a job as Apple's native solution, while providing value-added features that extend to family, friends, or groups of employees, so everyone can stop writing their computer's password on a sticky note, taped to the back of the keyboard – newsflash, it's not a "secret" if everyone knows to look there.

Login

Authenticating your Mac is a straightforward process. Enter your username (or select your account's name), enter your password and press the "Return" key to initiate the process. If the credentials are correct, you'll be granted access to the device and brought to the desktop screen.

Pretty simple, eh? Sure, it is. But it's not without its issues, namely, that anyone walking by or within eyeshot of your keyboard can easily watch you strike each key of your über complex password, remember it and later use it when you're not looking to access your computer – complete with all the rights and privileges that are bestowed upon your account. That's not good at all for security.

While not everyone has the photographic memory skills to remember long or exceptionally complex passwords, with the modern advancements in technology, namely, smartphones, threat actors can easily sit from afar while recording as you enter your credentials. This way, memory won't stand in the way of their gaining access to your precious data. Just replay the video, write down the password and use it against you, again, when you're not around.

Once again, Apple has you covered against shoulder surfing and related attacks that rely on physically observing end users entering their password in real-time. Enter biometrics, which we'll dive deeper into later within this chapter.

Additionally, users may wish to add a privacy filter to the monitor of their Mac for additional protection which filters indirect views, preventing anyone not standing directly in front of the screen from viewing what's being typed on screen.

System Preferences

If there's a location within macOS that allows users to set, modify, and manage groups of settings that directly impact how macOS behaves and thereby, affects the user experience, it's System Preferences.

From this single application, users can interface with macOS at a level that is not otherwise possible through other means. Think about certain customizations you prefer, like your desktop wallpaper or the type of screen saver that kicks in after several minutes of inactivity or where you can manage third-party devices, like mice, keyboards, printers, or large screen displays – all that and much more are managed through System Preferences.

It's also the same location where other preferences manage critical security settings for your Mac, like the creation of new user accounts, safeguarding passwords for accounts stored securely within macOS and granting access to Apple ID and iCloud accounts. This includes managing other critical security settings that could extend to your other devices, potentially including financial data stored within Wallet and Apple Pay.

Suffice it to say that the System Preferences app plays a significant role in the security of macOS and how your Mac operates. And while you need to sign into your Mac to gain access to this application, with a few notable exceptions, the multiple panes that make up the various sections contained within System Preferences are accessible to anyone with access to your session without restriction.

This means that if you leave your Apple computer unattended, anyone could easily launch the System Preferences app and wreak all sorts of havoc – like adding their fingerprint to Touch ID to login to your account later without knowing your password or modifying network sharing settings so they can access your personal and/or business data over the network without being anywhere near you physically. The list unfortunately is rife with risk to you and your data's security.

Thankfully, the developers at Apple considered this and included an optional setting to add a layer of security to all preference panes. Enabling it extends the locking mechanism, requiring users enter their admin credentials *each* time they wish to make a change to any preferences.

Set preferences pane to require an administrator password before changes are allowed

1. Launch System Preferences by navigating to Applications | System Preferences.app.

2. Click on Security & Privacy. Under the General tab, click the "Advanced…" button located in the bottom-right corner.

3. The advanced window will open. Check the box next to "Require an administrator password to unlock each System Preferences pane." Click the "OK" button to commit the changes. Then quit System Preferences.

The next time System Preferences is launched, regardless of the preference pane chosen, any configurable settings will appear opaque (or, greyed out) and the padlock located on the bottom-left of the window will be locked. Users are required to click the padlock once, then they'll be prompted to authenticate using admin-level credentials *before* access to modify any preference is granted.

User Account Types

When speaking about user accounts, most users want administrator-level access. By default, consumer users of most modern OS types are granted admin access when setting up their account initially, since it's important for the OS to have at least one administrator-type account to process tasks that require authorization, such as modifying system files when running updates, installing software and changing certain settings within your computer.

But what users sometimes fail to realize is that they don't *need* admin rights to use their computer for most day-to-day tasks. They *want* this access and while they may certainly feel as though they may be restricted from doing what they need to by not having it, apart from a few system-level tasks, users really don't need to be admins all the time.

When we get into enterprise environments where IT manages much, if not all, of a Mac's maintenance tasks, end users really don't need admin-level rights for anything.

Granting users permissions unnecessarily goes against the "principle of least privilege," which intends to provide all users – regardless of their role – the minimum level of rights necessary for them to complete their work. The rationale behind this is sound, if you take away an end user's ability to make changes to their Apple computer, this theoretically and technically will reduce the number of security issues that occur on that Mac.

The science behind the principle is sound: when a user is logged on to macOS, anything that occurs on that Mac does so within the context of their account and is limited to what access privileges are assigned to the account. So, if you're using the Guest account and trying to install software, this action is prevented from occurring because guest users do not have the proper permissions. If you're a standard Mac user account (i.e., non-administrator) and you happen to download some malicious software while browsing a website that's infected, the malware cannot modify system files since you'd be prompted to enter the credentials of a Mac user with admin permissions before the system files can be modified. The standard account's permissions will be denied access because they're not authorized.

To sum it up, while you may wish to have administrator access always at the ready when using a Mac – regardless of whether it's your personal computer or a company-owned one – it's always a best practice to use a standard-level account for your daily computing needs to minimize the damage that may stem from malware, suspicious software, or even risky behaviors.

On your personal Mac, when you need to perform an admin-level task, simply enter the administrator credentials you created when you initially set up your Mac and it will process that task without further inconvenience; for company-owned devices, IT administrators should take great care to keep the users with admin-level privileges to a minimum. An excellent way to mitigate potential risk while allowing those that require admin access to complete their job roles is to require the dual account approach recommended for the aforesaid consumer users.

On a related note, creating an administrator account to handle admin-level functions is straightforward enough, but creating one that is hidden to all users – except you – involves a few extra steps, but worth the effort, as it further enhances the security of your device by keeping the account effectively hidden on your Mac, appearing as though it doesn't even exist, while still providing you with the flexibility of using it when needed.

Create a new, hidden administrator account

Launch Terminal and enter the following command. When prompted, enter your admin credentials to execute the command that enables the ability to hide accounts:

```
sudo defaults write /Library/Preferences/com.apple.loginwindow
Hide500Users -bool YES
```

1. Launch System Preferences. Click on Users and Groups.

2. Click the padlock on the bottom-left corner (if locked) and enter your admin credentials to unlock access to preferences.

3. Click the "+" sign to add a new account. The New Account window will open. Select "Administrator" from the drop-down menu, provide a Full Name and Account Name, Password and Verify your password. Then click the "Create User" button to finalize creating your new admin account.

4. Next, right-click the newly created admin account name and select "Advanced Options..." from the context menu.

5. The Advanced Options menu will appear. Replace the three-digit number next to the User ID with another three-digit number under "499" (Ex. Type in "404").

6. Next to Home Directory, replace the path with "/var/username." Where the "username" should be the name of the newly created admin account. Click the "OK" button to commit changes.

7. Last, back at the Users and Groups preference page, select "Login Options" and select the radio button next to "Name and password," under the Display login window as section. Quit System Preferences.

When launching System Preferences, the next time you'll notice the admin account your credit and modified will no longer be displayed among the list of user accounts. This is an indicator that the account was created correctly, and the settings modified properly to hide it. Also, after the next logout, the login screen will display the username and password entry screen, further keeping your newly created admin account hidden from the login screen.

However, if your organization has IT and/or Security teams in place to manage devices administratively, then frankly, end users will likely not need administrator access for anything related to their productivity. In these cases, organizations would do well to provision only standard accounts for all users, while limiting administrator account access to only those maintenance-level tasks that require them, which IT and Security teams are already taking care of. This helps keep risk to a minimum, while allowing end users to focus on productivity – and not having to update their computers or perform any other IT-related tasks.

Multifactor Authentication

Referred to as MFA, for short, Apple also refers to this account security control as Two-Factor Authentication (2FA). The technology protects accounts from unauthorized access – even if your credentials are compromised – by relying on a secondary factor to verify your identity before authenticating the user and granting access to Apple services.

Before we get into how to enable 2FA, let's look at how it works and how it provides a huge benefit to users and organizations alike by protecting data and limiting access to restricted devices and resources.

Typical authentication works by relying on a factor. A factor refers to any of three possible pieces of evidence:

1. Something you know

2. Something you have

3. Something you are

When prompted by the authentication challenge, a user must provide the correct response as evidence that they are who they claim to be. Upon verifying the evidence, the system grants the user access to the system or resource they are requesting to use.

The first factor, something you know, is the most common type of evidence. Anyone that has ever been required to enter a username and password or numerical pin code to login to their computer or gain entry to a website is familiar with this factor.

The second factor, something you have, is less common but still a popular choice for access systems, particularly those that require presenting, swiping or tapping a card. This is identical to using a credit card when making a purchase or showing your ID card to show proof of age.

The third factor, something you are, relies on a physical trait or characteristic (biometrics) that is unique to the user to verify their identity, such as a fingerprint or scan of your retina. This factor has grown in popularity in recent years with the explosive growth of the mobile device market. Also, due to the difficulty in duplicating another user's distinctive signatures, biometrics has found a home in data protection schemes for information security.

Until 2FA or MFA is adopted, the security protocol in use for safeguarding computer access is based on only one factor being selected. Typically, this means the first factor – protecting access through a username and password. However, when 2FA/MFA is implemented, access becomes protected by any two factors from the preceding list, requiring users to verify their identity in both ways – not just one – before they're granted access to the resource being requested.

For example, Apple's iCloud service requires something you know and something you have, to better safeguard your data, once 2FA is enabled. If you wish to access data or services protected by iCloud, you must first authenticate using your iCloud account and password. If successful, you will be prompted to enter a code that is sent to your personal, trusted device (like an iPhone). The authentication process will halt temporarily until this code is entered. If correct, authentication completes successfully and you are granted access to iCloud's resources; if incorrect, the process ends, failing authentication and thereby being denied access to iCloud resources.

How to enable 2FA for iCloud

1. On your Mac, go to System Preferences | Apple ID. Click on Password & Security from the sidebar.

2. Next to the Two-Factor Authentication section, it should read "Off," indicating the service is not enabled. Click the "Turn On..." button to enable the service.

3. From here, you'll be prompted to enter a phone number to receive the verification code that is sent to register your smartphone for the first time.

4. Upon receiving the verification code on your phone, enter it into the verification window on your Mac.

Once the process is completed, your iPhone and phone number will be registered as trusted devices within your iCloud account, allowing you to receive the 2FA verification codes that are sent each time you attempt to access your iCloud account.

If you don't have an Apple iPhone or simply use an older device that doesn't support 2FA, don't fret. Apple also supports Two-Step Verification,[1] which is similar to 2FA, except it relies on different methods for the trust and delivery of verification codes and does not provide the streamlined user experience that is built into modern versions of macOS, iOS, and watchOS.[2]

FileVault

Storage encryption. The Alamo or, more to the point, the last bastion of data security that keeps your sensitive data private and away from unauthorized access to anyone without the decryption key.

---

[1] https://support.apple.com/en-us/HT204152

[2] https://support.apple.com/en-us/HT204915

In macOS, the disk encryption technology that Apple uses is called FileVault 2. In Chapter 7, we covered how the underlying technology works, including the algorithms and cipher strength used to secure your private data. While the original FileVault technology only encrypted the user's home folder, FileVault 2 encrypts the entire volume for greater protection. The term FileVault is used interchangeably by Apple to refer to the disk encryption technology, so when you read FileVault throughout the rest of this chapter, it's referring to the modern version – FileVault 2 – found on current versions of macOS.

And as is the case with other Apple-developed technologies, FileVault conforms to Apple's design principles, meaning it's easy to enable and dead simple to use. The decryption of your data is tied directly to your Mac account, so when you (or a FileVault-enabled user) successfully authenticate to macOS, the authorized account decrypts the disk, allowing the user access to the files stored in their respective home directory. When your Mac is powered off – data is scrambled and therefore unreadable *until* an authorized user successfully enters their credentials.

Should anyone that is **not** authorized to read any personal and/or work-related data stored on your Apple computer, or in the event that your Mac gets lost or stolen, you can rest assured that the integrity and confidentiality of the data stored on the disk will remain encrypted. As a matter of fact, even mounting the drive as an external disk, removing the drive on Macs with end user removable disks or booting the Mac to another OS (see the Startup section in Chapter 7) keeps the data on the drive unreadable to anyone without the decryption key or authorized user account.

That's why it was referred to earlier as The Alamo, it's the last line of defense from bad actors and anyone else fixing to steal your data. So, let's walk through the steps to enable FileVault, shall we?

How to enable FileVault

1. Launch System Preferences.

2. Click on Security & Privacy | FileVault.

3. Click on the small padlock (if locked) to unlock the preference settings menu.

4. With the FileVault settings unlocked, click on the "Turn On FileVault..." button to begin the process.

That's it! Once FileVault is enabled, the encryption process will begin in the background so as to not interrupt the user while they're working. Once the process is complete, the Mac will require a reboot to finalize it. After the restart, the disk will be encrypted and require an authorized user's account (or the recovery key) to unlock it.

Oh, and about the recovery key. A recovery key is used as a backup option to unlock the disk should the user forget their password, or the account gets locked out. The recovery key will be displayed on-screen when FileVault is initially enabled and should be stored in a secure place away from anyone you do not wish to have access to unlocking the disk on your Mac.

A better and more secure option is possible if you have an iCloud account. When the recovery key is created, macOS will detect that an iCloud account is logged in and prompt the user to accept or deny securely storing the recovery key within the cloud-based account. By agreeing to this, if the recovery key is ever required to unlock the disk, simply login to iCloud and the key will automatically be retrieved, unlocking the disk in the process. When prompted, select the radio button next to "Allow my iCloud account to unlock my disk" and click the "Continue" button to proceed.

For enterprise users managing devices through a Mobile Device Management (MDM) solution (covered in Chapter 9), Apple's security frameworks establish provisions for managing the automation and enforcement of FileVault.

This includes a mechanism for automatically generating and storing the recovery key securely within the device's record in the MDM for future use – no relying on writing or storing unique keys for hundreds or thousands of devices necessary.

One last note, if the account password is forgotten, the recovery key is lost, the user wants to reset their account password or simply wishes to regenerate the recovery key, FileVault will need to be disabled. Repeating the steps to enable it, as shown earlier, will allow the user to make any changes during the re-enabling process.

Screen Saver

Anyone that's ever used a computer of any kind should be familiar with the function of the screen saver. After all, the definition lies in its name: it saves your screen from artifacts and burn-in due to static images being displayed for a period of time.

Standard stuff to be sure, but what some macOS users don't know is that there is a way to force your Mac to require the user enter their credentials when the screen saver kicks in.

Enabling this feature achieves two security functions:

1. By requiring authentication to wake your Mac, it keeps data safe from unauthorized users, preventing data from being accessed.

2. The screen saver function can be triggered at any time – not just at the requisite timeout period – by using Hot Corners to invoke screen lock to protect your system anytime you need to step away.

Enable password requirement for screen saver

1. In System Preferences, click on the Security & Privacy pane.

2. Check the box next to Require password after sleep or screen saver begins and select the timeout from the drop-down menu. For the best security, selecting "Immediately" requires the password as soon as the screen saver kicks in.

Enable the Screen Saver

1. Launch System Preferences and click on the Desktop & Screen Saver pane.

2. Check the box next to Show screen saver after and select the desired timeout in minutes.

Enable Hot Corners trigger

1. In System Preferences, click on the Desktop and Screen Saver pane.

2. Click on the "Hot Corners..." button to bring up the settings.

3. In the new window, select any of the four screen corners as the zone that will trigger the desired action when the mouse scrolls to that area.

4. On new versions of macOS, from the drop-down menu in the chosen corner, select "Lock Screen," then click the "OK" button to commit changes. On older versions of macOS, select the "Start Screen Saver" action to invoke the lock screen immediately when the screen saver begins.

By combining these three preceding sections, you'll now have the protection of keeping your screen free from the damaging effects of static imagery, while keeping data safe from bad actors with physical access to your computer by requiring a password each time the screen saver begins

Furthermore, the Hot Corners function can be called upon at any time – not just when the screensaver times out – by dragging the mouse cursor to the selected screen corner. This permits users to quickly and easily lock their screens when having to step away from their Mac computer without the need to log out, while keeping the contents of their session intact and secured.

Lock Screen

Introduced in macOS Big Sur, Apple included the feature to lock your screen to secure your Mac. This feature continues to exist in subsequent versions of macOS to immediately lock the screen before stepping away from your logged in session to prevent unauthorized users or bad actors from accessing your data or manipulating your session.

Similar to the previous section, where we discussed invoking the screen saver and the use of hot corners, the lock screen function is also available as one of the choices that users may perform immediately to lock their Mac.

There are several other methods that users can use to lock their screen besides the use of hot corners, depending on the type of Mac they're using.

Manually lock the screen from the Apple menu

1. Click on the Apple menu and select "Lock Screen" from the menu.

Lock screen using Touch ID button

1. If your Mac comes with the built-in Touch ID button or a Magic Keyboard with the included technology, simply press the button once to instantly lock your computer.

Locking your screen with a keyboard shortcut

1. Press the Control, Command and Q keys at the same time to immediately lock your screen from your keyboard.

Conversely, unlocking your Mac computer's locked screen is as simple as

- Entering your **password**.

- Using the Touch ID button.

- Securely pairing your Apple Watch.

Malware Protection

Apple's developers include security software, like malware protection, that's built-in to macOS to keep Mac safeguarded from known malware threats.

There are a number of technologies Apple has baked right into macOS to ensure that users, devices, and data remain free from malware threats. All the technologies are intrinsically integrated into all aspects of macOS to provide broad protection coverage throughout the operating system.

Furthermore, they work mostly in the background to keep Mac safeguarded without impacting the user experience that Apple is known to deliver. Also, due to the tight integration, Apple regularly updates these technologies and signature files used to detect current and newly discovered malware independent of macOS update cadence, ensuring your Apple devices always have the most current protection against known malware threats that target Mac.

Let's meet these software-based technologies,[3] shall we?

---

[3] https://support.apple.com/guide/security/protecting-against-malware-sec469d47bd8/web

- **XProtect**: Antivirus technology that relies on signature-based definitions to identify and prevent malware. The definitions used by Apple are called YARA rules,[4] which stands for Yet Another Ridiculous Acronym. The rule-based approach creates descriptions of malware families based on patterns familiar to each family. By including text and/or binary patterns within the rules, each rule can aid in identifying a class of malware by matching scanned files for matches to the strings and Boolean expressions. If a match is found, XProtect knows it has detected malware and moves to prevent it from compromising your Mac.

- **Malware Removal Tool (MRT)**: A system-level application bundle whose job is to automatically remove malicious software from your Mac – cleanly and safely – without further impact to macOS or the end user. It's also known to remove potentially unwanted and/or malicious Safari extensions, as well.

- **Notarization**: Apple's scanning service to detect malware in macOS applications that are distributed outside of the App Store. It's a two-part process, the first of which works by scanning apps submitted by developers for known malware. If free of malicious code, Apple issues the developer a notarization ticket specifically for the verified app. The developer then includes that ticket with their app when distributing it so that users are ensured that the app is free from known malware.

---

[4] https://en.wikipedia.org/wiki/YARA

- **Gatekeeper**: The second part of the process is Gatekeeper, which obtains its name by checking apps upon first run (and after being updated) for the existence of a notarization ticket. This service verifies that the ticket is both active and tied to the specific app being launched, to give users peace of mind that the app has been vetted by Apple to ensure it does not include malicious code. If an app is found to contain malicious code, Apple can revoke the ticket so that when Gatekeeper performs verification, it will prevent the app from running.

- **App Store**: The first-party store distributes apps that have been submitted by first- and third-party developers to Apple. Apple scans software prior to approving apps for distribution to ensure they are free from malicious code or infringe on user privacy without their knowledge. But also, by hosting developer's apps within Apple's cloud, they assure users that apps have not been modified in any way, ensuring users are always downloading clean software applications each time.

- **App Sandbox**[5]: Also referred to as containerization in cybersecurity, this technology effectively restricts how apps are run in the background so as to limit access to system sources and user data in the event that an app becomes compromised. This works to contain the potential damage to the system and user data, keeping it to a minimum.

---

[5] https://developer.apple.com/documentation/security/app_sandbox

- **Transparency, Consent and Control (TCC)**[6]: In line with Apple's privacy frameworks and principles, TCC reinforces the belief that users should have full control over what apps are doing with all aspects of their data. To do so, the model enforces the system requirement ensuring that all apps must obtain consent from the user *prior* to accessing files in local and network directories. TCC also extends to apps interacting with data, such as accessing photos, recording video from the webcam, and listening to audio through the microphone to name but a few resources. We go into further detail regarding TCC later in this chapter.

Firewall

As we discussed, macOS offers numerous security features to keep data safe from threat actors locally **and** over the network. One of the best ways to keep Macs safe over the network is the Firewall.

Firewall technology is a cornerstone of network-based protection throughout computing. Whether it's hardware- or software-based, Firewalls work by controlling access to resources over network connections. Typically, Firewalls can manage access to websites and network locations based on IP address or entire IP ranges. Also, blocking services and furthering security by identifying and preventing known types of attacks used by bad actors to test device security, gather information about a host or detect open ports that may provide attackers an open door to communicate with your device.

---

[6] https://support.apple.com/guide/security/controlling-app-access-to-files-secddd1d86a6/web

Successfully configuring and managing Firewall settings and traffic requires intimate knowledge of networking and security concepts that go beyond the scope of this book. However, for the purposes of safeguarding your Mac, Apple's implementation of Firewall technology isn't as complex, so it doesn't require a degree in cybersecurity in order for users to gain the benefit of securing network communications through its simple, easy-to-use interface.

Enabling the Firewall on your Mac

1. Launch System Preferences. Click on Security & Privacy, then click on the Firewall tab to access the preference pane.

2. Next, click the "Turn On Firewall..." button to enable Firewall protection.

By default, the macOS Firewall will protect against incoming network-based threats automatically without further user intervention. However, if you wish to enable greater protection, click on the "Firewall Options..." button to bring up optional configurations to strengthen network security.

To maximize network security, there are several options available from "Firewall Options..." within the Security & Privacy preference pane. These can be configured independently – or all together – to customize security to best suit your needs. In the case of enterprise organizations, IT administrators can manage these Firewall settings by configuring them to enforce protections without compromising the user's experience.

- **Block all incoming connections**: As the name implies, all incoming network connections – except those required to establish and maintain basic access to the Internet – are blocked when this box is checked. The benefit to this setting being enabled is that nearly all incoming connections are barred from making connections to Mac. A possible downside, however, is that services and/or apps you rely upon to remain productive may also be blocked.

- **Automatically allow signed software to receive incoming connections**: Apps that are signed by the developer and pass Gatekeeper's notarization verification are automatically allowed to receive incoming connections when this box is checked. This prevents unsigned apps that may be running on your Mac – with or without your knowledge – from receiving incoming network communications.

- **Enable stealth mode**: Different from the first selection, when this box is checked, only communications that are used to test network connectivity are blocked. For example, the Ping command, which is a small network utility that tests the connectivity of one computer with another. Often, this serves as the first line of a larger attack chain with bad actors using this to determine if a device is online and communicating.

The last setting under Firewall Options is the application list. Users and IT administrators can manage whether incoming connections are allowed or blocked, based on individual applications and service types. For example, if you wish to allow iTunes access to receive incoming connections so that music can be updated dynamically, clicking on the "+" icon allows users to add the app and set the permissions to allow. At the same time, if a torrent client needs to be blocked, adding that app to the list and setting the permissions to "Block incoming connections" will actively prevent that app from communicating over the network.

A good rule of thumb for the applications list is to curate your list of the apps and services that require incoming access enabled, that might be a great place to start.

Conversely, if there are apps that you know for a fact you would like blocked, curating a list of those apps helps users coordinate between the critical apps and services they're sure require access and those that should be blocked. This leaves any other apps and services you may be unsure of for later until you've had an opportunity to vet them more thoroughly without impacting your experience too much.

VPN

Most users, especially those that use Mac for business are surely familiar with VPN. For those that aren't or simply need a refresher, VPN stands for Virtual Private Networking and that is the name given to the technology that is used to secure network connections when users need to access company resources securely.

At least, that's the basic definition of enterprise VPN. For personal or consumer VPN software, the definition takes on a slightly different meaning that leans more into preserving user privacy by masking what websites are visited and services used by encrypting the traffic transmitted over network connection while providing a masked IP address as well.

Regardless of whether the intention is secure business or personal traffic, the endgame is the same – security is the name of the game, and VPN technology does an admirable job of keeping data secure.

macOS, by default, does not provide the networking infrastructure necessary to enable VPN protection, but it does contain the necessary components to support various types of VPN technologies.

Because of this, most of the time using VPN relies on a third-party service provider to provide the requisite networking details that you can use to configure VPN support within macOS to gain these protective benefits for data and privacy, respectively.

While I won't go into rating or recommending VPN service providers, since there are many reputable websites on the Internet that do a superb job of breaking down multiple services based on user feedback, features included, and pricing model, I will say that unequivocally, VPN services are highly recommended for anyone that uses the Internet for anything related to personal uses from public or untrusted Wi-Fi hotspots. For business-related tasks, while working remotely, upgrade this recommendation to absolutely must to keep data secure while in transit and shielded away from potentially prying eyes.

For users that would like to gain some of the privacy benefits of VPN without subscribing to a monthly service, Apple offers iCloud Private Relay. Though it is not a substitute for full-blown VPN service, it provides user privacy protections similar to VPN and if you already have an iCloud account, it's free! As of this writing, the service has been in beta testing for quite some time, but it is open to iCloud users to freely test (more on this and other iCloud services later in this chapter).

Zero Trust

A relative newcomer to the cybersecurity space, though it has existed in some form for some time, this newer technology is more geared toward enterprise business use to protect data while safeguarding privacy.

If this sounds eerily like an enterprise VPN, you'd be right. In fact, while VPN offers decent security protections for personal use, business use cases have evolved due to migration to remote and hybrid work environments alongside the widespread adoption of mobile devices, like tablets and smartphones.

This transformation has made VPN's legacy protections unsuitable because it's not able to provide the levels of security that are required from modern computing when compared to today's threat landscape.

Enter Zero Trust. The security model that draws upon the very best of VPN, while eliminating the negatives. See the following breakdown for a better understanding of how Zero Trust succeeds where VPN fails:

	Pros	Cons
VPN	• Secures connections made to remote resources over the network.	• Grants users permission to the entire network, not just what's needed.
	• Encrypts data in transit.	• Protection must be manully turned on each time it is used.
	• Preserves user privacy.	• Introduces latency which slows down network speeds.
	• Provides anonimity online by masking IP address.	• Uses more bandwidth as network traffic must be backhauled through corporate network.
		• Increased adminitrative management from maintaining network equipment.
		• Complex configurations required or risk of data leakage possible.
		• Relies on seprate account access, meaning a secondary set of credentials to secure data.
		• If account access is compromised, access to all resources are compromised.
		• Service does not support all OS and device types.

(continued)

	Pros	Cons
Zero Trust	• All the benefits available to VPN.	• None of the drawbacks to VPN.
	• Adheres to principle of least privilege, granting users access to only the minimum number of resources they need to be productive.	• Depending on organizational needs and equipment, Zero Trust may not be feasable without upgrading upgrading equipment, modifying workflows and/or updating policies.
	• Protections are always enabled and do not require users to turn on services while preventing users from turning off services.	
	• Utilizes minimal resources, reducing impact to network speeds, the device or user experience.	
	• Cloud-based infrastructure means IT customizes access policies -- not manage equipment or complex software.	
	• Integrates with cloud-based identity providers, leveraging SSO and MFA for greater authentication security.	
	• Creates microtunnels for each unique connection, keeping access to apps/ services isloated from one another. If one becomes compromised, simply deny access to the affected app/service without impacting others. Effectively prevents lateral network movements	
	• Supports all modern OS's, device types and network connections.	

For enterprise users and IT admins alike, Zero Trust marks the current state of information security and represents what organizations should be aiming for to protect data against modern threats. For personal users, Zero Trust isn't as feasible a solution since it relies on several components that many services simply do not support at the consumer-grade levels.

But this shouldn't prevent users from striving to best secure themselves, their devices and, of course, their data.

iCloud

Long ago, Apple had the idea to develop a cloud-based infrastructure that it would use to handle the web-based traffic generated from Apple devices communicating with Apple to obtain service updates (notifications), download apps and media content, store user photos, send/receive emails, and many other features supported under the iCloud moniker.

To achieve this, Apple built several large data centers throughout the world to speed the delivery of data to users globally. As of this writing, there are purportedly almost a dozen of these campuses as they tend to call them with more in the various planning stages of being built to handle the collective throughput from user's device requests.

However, the aim of this book isn't to discuss Apple's expansion plans. No, it's securing your Mac and how to do so in a way that provides the greatest protection to data, while preserving user privacy, without impacting the user experience. To that end, iCloud offers personal and professional users a great deal of protective services that are all optional, but highly recommended as they not only shift the technical burden from the user to Apple's shoulders, allowing you to choose what needs protecting – Apple takes care of the rest.

Before we dive into iCloud services, first we touch upon some of the technologies[7] – some of which you'll recognize – that Apple has implemented or made available to provide best-in-class security to protect your data and preserve your privacy.

- **Data security**: Data is encrypted both while in transit and while at rest to and from Apple's data centers.

- **End-to-end encryption**: Apple services, such as Messages, rely on this form of encryption between the sender's device and the recipient's device means any information exchanged is kept only between those two users – even Apple cannot see what's being sent/received – as the encryption keys are derived from the individual devices and each user's respective device passcode.

- **Two-factor authentication**: 2FA is the technology covered earlier in this chapter that prompts users to provide verification of their identity through a secondary factor before access is granted to a resource.

- **Access policies**: Certain data types may be regulated, such as Health data, meaning that it's legally protected to be managed only by the patient and those they explicitly authorize. To back up Health data, backups must have encryption enabled. If not, this type of data is omitted from the backup process to preserve privacy.

- **Recovery**: To aid users in recovering their lost data, Apple offers several options. iCloud Data Recovery Service[8] helps recover data stored within iCloud, such

---

[7] https://support.apple.com/en-us/HT202303
[8] https://support.apple.com/en-us/HT212516

as photos or music by resetting your account. End-to-end encrypted services, however, are not recoverable through this option. If you have a trusted contact you authorize, they can be selected to help you recover access to iCloud data should you ever get locked out. A final solution is the account recovery key,[9] which is a 28-character code that helps users who've been locked out reset their password or regain access to their Apple ID.

Let's look at some select iCloud services, how they're secured, and why they're important to sustaining the security of your Mac:

Keychain: As discussed in a previous section within this chapter on passwords, Keychain saves all of the accounts and passwords authorized by users securely using end-to-end encryption. Not only does this provide password management functionality but natively stores this data securely so that only you – the user – can access it.

Private Relay[10]: One of the newer features Apple introduced as part of expanded services titled iCloud+. This feature protects the user's privacy when using Safari, specifically the data that is transmitted within web traffic as part of the usual process of requesting access to a website.

Let me explain. Typically, when a user requests to view a website, the natural exchange of data in this process exposes potentially identifiable information, such as the DNS records and IP address. By itself, this data is concerning, but as more of this data is gathered over time, it can – and sadly is sometimes – used by bad actors to build a profile of the user's location and browsing history.

These profiles can and often do get sold to organizations that use it to market services targeted to users, among other more concerning uses.

---

[9] https://support.apple.com/en-us/HT208072
[10] https://support.apple.com/en-us/HT212614

But Private Relay works to halt the leaking of web data by ensuring that requests are sent through two separate and secure Internet relays.

The first request is made using your IP address, which is already visible to your ISP and the first relay, managed by Apple. Your DNS records are encrypted and sent to the first relay. The second relay is managed by a third-party provider as they generate a temporary IP address, decrypt the website requested and connect the user to the site in real-time.

At any given time, the separate relays only have a portion of the decrypted data while the other has just an encrypted portion. Meaning your web data is never together and unencrypted at the same time with any of the relays.

For additional anonymity, Private Relay may be configured to generate a temporary IP address based on your generalized location or made to be more ambiguous by utilizing one from a pool based on the country and time zone from your location.

Hide My Email[11]: Since the previous service protects web data, it's only fitting that this service protects email privacy when using Safari and in Mail.app.

It achieves this by creating a random email address that acts as a forwarder to your real email account. This protects your real email address from being shared when filling out a form, registering for a new service or subscribing to a newsletter to name a few instances where this feature helps to keep your real email address from third parties that may potentially spam or sell your data without your consent.

Best of all is that since this service is integrated directly into both Safari and Mail, when you're prompted to enter your email address in the former or manually creating a new message in the latter, Hide My Email will prompt you when clicking on the From field if you'd like to use the service.

---

[11] https://support.apple.com/guide/mac-help/use-hide-my-email-mchle62f7f45/mac

Every time a new recipient is to be messaged, the service will walk you through the brief process of generating a random email to use so each email is unique and tied to that particular recipient. If Hide My Email has already created an email for that recipient, it will automatically enter that address in the From field for you.

It also offers a management option to view the different emails created and which recipients they're connected to. If you no longer wish to communicate with that recipient, simply delete the entry and emails they send to the temporary account will no longer arrive in your inbox.

iCloud Drive: Cloud storage is not a new concept per se, but iCloud Drive provides users a means of essentially rolling their own cloud storage that is both tied to their iCloud account and natively integrated into macOS unlike any other service provider. Furthermore, you can rest assured that your data is encrypted – both in transit and on the server – using a minimum 128-bit AES encryption cipher.

Moreover, thanks to the deep integration with macOS and first- and third-party applications, when creating, editing, and saving data from supported applications, they can all be stored directly within iCloud Drive and shared across all your Apple-centric devices and updated in real-time.

But wait, there's more! iCloud offers multiple service tiers beyond the free offering. Higher tiers include additional storage space – all the way up to 2TB. This means that macOS users can enable storing their data within iCloud Drive, such that macOS will copy data located in the Desktop and Documents folders, respectively, to iCloud Drive, permitting secure access and storage of your data.[12]

This requires a stable connection to the Internet of course, but Apple has thought of that as well by implementing an offline mode. Simply put, tapping the download button (see the cloud with the arrow pointing down) to download a copy of the file to your Mac locally. There, you can

---

[12] https://support.apple.com/en-us/HT201104

edit the document as needed offline without any interruption, and when Internet access is reestablished, all changes will automatically be uploaded to iCloud Drive.

Find My Mac: The "Find My..." service included with iCloud plays a critical role in helping users find their Apple device in the event that it should become lost or, worse, stolen. Though disabled by default, users will be prompted to enable it (and the Location Services it relies upon) during the initial Setup of their Mac and when logging in with their iCloud account the first time.[13]

However, that's not all this service does. Find My Mac also provides users with the ability to lock and wipe or erase their Mac after it's been lost or stolen. While you might be thinking, "if I lost my Mac, I'd want to get it back" – and that's a completely rational thought and reaction to having your precious Mac and all the data contained therein taken away.

But consider for a second the possibility that your Mac is unrecoverable. As difficult a pill as that is to swallow, it's definitely a possibility. So, with that in mind, your personal and/or work data are still on that Mac. How would you feel if someone else, a stranger let's say, was able to gain access to your data and read your messages, gather sensitive company documents, view your photos, and access your web history?

We all have private lives. The key word there being private, as in, no one else's business unless you make it so. In cases where Macs are lost or stolen, that option is sometimes taken away from the user.

Find My Mac offers users a shot at getting their devices back through physically tracking it. Should that fail or simply prove untenable (say, if the device is located on another continent, for example), there is a second option at maintaining the security of your data while preserving your privacy – remotely wipe the device.[14]

---

[13] https://support.apple.com/guide/findmy-mac/set-up-fmm53101237/mac
[14] https://support.apple.com/guide/findmy-mac/erase-a-device-fmmbe7bb71f4/mac

Issuing the wipe command remotely allows iCloud to send your lost/ stolen Mac a command that, upon the Mac receiving the command, will cause the Apple computer to erase all data from the local storage drive permanently.

Is this the most desirable outcome? No. But it is a better alternative to possibly having personal and/or business data exposed to unauthorized users or worse – distributed among the public at large. In fact, some organizations create policies to require this type of response when devices are lost to limit liability and/or ensure compliance with regulatory oversight.

Mac App Store

The Mac App Store was designed to securely host and distribute applications created by Apple and third-party developers for macOS. While developers that wish to have their apps distributed through Apple's built-in app store must comply with the developer requirements imposed by Apple, the process to have your apps hosted by Apple begins with paid membership into Apple's Developer Program.[15]

Not only does membership permit developers to submit their apps for hosting, but Apple provides a number of tools and services to aid in the development of apps, while providing a secure environment – free from tampering and malicious code – for devs and users alike. Furthermore, once approved for hosting within Apple's global content delivery network (CDN), devs can rest assured that their apps are accessible securely from anywhere around the world, with Apple handling the financial transactions, if your apps are not free, for a nominal fee of the sales.

---

[15] https://developer.apple.com/programs/

Also included are dashboards to support devs in determining metrics, such as product page views, sales, installations, etc. This being a book predominantly about securing your Mac, we're going to circle back to the security-focused aspects and benefits of the Mac App Store.

Like I mentioned before, the Mac App Store scans all apps for malicious code that could potentially harm your Mac. Apps distributed through the app store are also signed and notarized, meaning that it's routinely checked by Gatekeeper to ensure that the app hasn't had its notarization ticket revoked due to the existence of malware or other such malicious code.

Since Apple has designed its CDN technology with security and privacy in mind, app store apps are secured against tampering, meaning threat actors would have an incredibly difficult time accessing the protected cloud-based storage **and** compromising the integrity of hosted apps *without* Apple's knowledge. This adds confidence to the users downloading and installing app store-hosted programs, knowing there are layers of mitigative strategies in place to scan for, detect, and remediate the presence of compromised software.

Another benefit is that apps hosted are always the latest versions of that app. So, say a developer uploads v1.0 of their app and says the app is installed on your Mac and working perfectly. After some time, the developer releases a new update, let's call it v1.2 with new features. After it has been scanned and approved for hosting within the app store, the user will receive a notification alert from the Mac App Store that the app in question has a pending update available.

In managed environments, like corporate-owned devices, IT admins have additional control over app deployment and upgrade cycles, by enabling a feature within their mobile device management (MDM) software to require the latest version of an app to always be downloaded and installed. By doing so, Mac App Store provisioned apps will automatically be kept up-to-date each time a new version is made available – without requiring users or IT further intervention.

Lastly, a somewhat overlooked benefit to security and user privacy is the brand recognition of the Apple Mac App Store. While recognition alone doesn't keep macOS safe from threats of course, but the fact that there exist third-party or unauthorized app stores available helps steer users toward the real app store managed by Apple and away from unknown app stores that are potentially managed by threat actors or simply have no oversight, meaning that apps found in those rogue stores could be hosting a mix of fake versions of real apps and real apps that have been cracked, or had their internal security broken, lending itself to be modified by bad actors seeking to infect your Mac, compromise your data, and/or obtain your privacy information – or all of the above.

Secure Memory

Also known as secure virtual memory,[16] this function gets its name from how computing systems (Mac included) will often offload some of the data that is waiting to be processed or being sent back to an app after processing. Typically, this "waiting room" exists between the CPU and the operating system, with data essentially waiting its place in line within RAM (the computer's hardware memory component).

Sometimes though, multiple apps open equally more threads pre- and post-processing than the RAM can handle. In these cases, to prevent the system from grinding to a halt, OS, like macOS utilize some available storage from the hard disk or solid-state disk and use that free space to offload anything that spills over from RAM. This spillover is called virtual memory, since it operates much like RAM, but is facilitated by permanent storage which isn't as fast as the hardware memory components used for RAM. But it does the trick just the same.

---

[16] https://support.apple.com/guide/mac-help/what-is-secure-virtual-memory-on-mac-mh11852/mac

By default, when macOS goes to sleep because the user closes the lid on their MacBook laptop or presses the power button on the keyboard, the contents that are currently stored within RAM are written to additional disk space, creating virtual memory. The original copy of this data is kept both suspended within RAM and a backup copy is stored as virtual memory. Should something cause a copy to become unavailable, there is a temporary backup available so that data loss does not occur.

Data stored in RAM is secure, plus it requires specialized knowledge to extract and physical access to obtain. While it's not impossible to gather, it definitely presents more of a challenge than the much simpler alternative: obtaining the backup stored within virtual memory.

As we covered before, when FileVault is enabled, the entire volume is encrypted – this includes virtual memory – on HFS+ formatted volumes. On APFS formatted volumes, a separate partition for virtual memory is created and automatically encrypted. However, when Mac is put to sleep, a copy of the FileVault key exists within RAM, so anyone with physical access to your Mac could obtain a copy of the data contained within virtual memory without needing to reauthorize themselves with FileVault. Apple security engineers have considered this and provided a way to both clear the RAM's contents before going to sleep and secure virtual memory to eliminate this threat vector.

The solution requires a two-step command process, the first of which will disable the default "hybrid sleep" configuration in favor of the full "hibernation" mode.

View current mode and enable full hibernation

1. Launch Terminal.

2. Enter the following command to view current settings:

   ```
   pmset -g | grep -e 'hibernatemode'
   ```

3. macOS has multiple configuration settings available for various sleep modes. These modes correspond to the following values:

135

0 = RAM powered while sleeping.

3 = RAM powered and written to disk (default setting).

25 = RAM contents written to disk and not powered.

To set the most secure mode with a value of '25', enter the following command:

```
sudo pmset 'hibernatemode' 25
```

Set FileVault key delete on hibernate

1. Launch Terminal and enter the following command:

```
sudo pmset destroyfvkeystandby 1
```

Once both commands have been processed successfully, Mac will copy the contents of RAM to virtual memory then clear the RAM and delete the FileVault key from memory. This will secure virtual memory by requiring that user's unlock disk access upon authenticating again.

There are a few possible downsides to the more stringent security controls. Namely, by purging the RAM of its contents, when Mac wakes from sleep, it does so a bit slower than when the contents remain in RAM. This is due to an additional step in waking from the hibernation process that macOS must copy the contents from secure virtual memory back to the RAM. It won't take minutes, but for some users, the additional few seconds are noticeable. Additionally, maintenance wakes and Apple's Power Nap feature (on supported Macs with flash-based drives) will be effectively disabled due to the new configuration.

Transparency, Consent and Control (TCC)

The TCC controls built-in to macOS are designed to provide end users the ability to determine and manage how apps, services, and websites access, gather, interact with, and use their private data.

Located in System Preferences | Security & Privacy within the Privacy tab, the aim of this part of the Apple Endpoint Security Framework (ESF) is to help users manage their information that Mac makes available to third-parties on a network and across the internet.

TCC is made up of several categories,[17] each pertaining to a particular feature, function, or resource within macOS. By clicking on a specific category, a list of apps that have requested authorization to use that resource is available, alongside the status of that request. A checkmark next to the app or service's name means authorization has been granted, while no checkmark means authorization was denied.

- Location Services
- Contacts
- Calendars
- Reminders
- Photos
- Camera
- Microphone
- Speech Recognition
- Accessibility
- Input Monitoring
- Full Disk Access
- Files and Folders
- Screen Recording
- Media & Apple Music

---

[17] https://support.apple.com/guide/mac-help/change-privacy-preferences-on-mac-mh32356/mac

- HomeKit

- Bluetooth

- User Availability

- Automation

- Developer Tools

- Analytics & Improvements

- Apple Advertising

Generally speaking, the categories are self-explanatory, like Camera referring to apps that have requested access to use the Mac's built-in webcam. Others still aren't so straightforward, like Files & Folders, which includes a list of apps that have requested access to your Mac's file system folders, but may vary depending on which folders were accessed when trying to open a file. For example, if trying to open a spreadsheet document saved to your Desktop folder, the app listed may have a checkmark next to the Desktop folder; however, the Documents and/or Downloads folder may remain unchecked. This means the app is permitted to access files from your Desktop but denied access from the Documents and Downloads directories, respectively.

Manually granting permissions is as easy as checking the box to allow access rights while unchecking the box denies access rights. Pretty simple, no? Most of the time, though, users will be prompted to approve or deny when an app, service, or website first requests to utilize a resource. This is a fairly common operating procedure and helps keep users productive without having to toggle back to System Preferences each time.

Since users can accumulate many requests over time and, worse yet, some of the authorizations could include software no longer used, it is important for users to regularly visit the Privacy tab and scan each category for any permissions granted that are no longer useful or necessary. Each unnecessary permission left enabled represents a small but significant hole poked into your Mac's defenses. Clearing out any authorizations that are no longer valid helps to strengthen your Mac and preserve your privacy by denying access to *your* data.

Touch ID

Initially mentioned in the Passwords section of this chapter, Touch ID's advanced technology[18] is used to secure access to systems and data through the use of physical features that uniquely identify an individual. The features that make up biometrics are extremely difficult to replicate as they are associated with physical traits unique to each user. For example, a person's fingerprint is a perfect example and, coincidentally, the most used trait in biometrics since no two fingerprints are considered a scientifically identical match to one another.

Another example is the iris scan, which takes several pictures of a user's eyeball and utilizes algorithms to detail and quantify the individual grooves and markers within the iris, creating a computational pattern that is then referenced each time a user submits to retinal scanning. If a match is determined, access is granted; but if no match is made, access remains denied.

Apple relies on two technologies: Touch ID and Face ID for their biometrics implementation to secure user access to data. However, as of this writing, only Touch ID – based on fingerprint-based biometrics – has been implemented within macOS-based computing devices. The latter, Face ID, uses a 3D-scan of the user's facial features to provide this form of biometrics protection. As of this writing, Apple limits this form of biometrics only to devices based on iOS.

---

[18] https://support.apple.com/en-us/HT204587

Among the security features included in macOS, Touch ID represents the crux of several forms of protection, namely:

- Authentication

- Encryption

- Financial

By default, Touch ID is not enabled not because it's an oversight, mind you, but because before it can be enabled, Apple requires a few security protections to be in place first. These prerequisites are:

- Apple computer that supports Secure Enclave

- User account and password

- Touch ID setup completed

Once you've met the first two requirements, the third one can be accomplished by following the prompts to enable Touch ID and start protecting your Mac with Apple's advanced security technology.

How to enable Touch ID

1. Login onto your Mac with your account.

2. Launch System Preferences | Touch ID.

3. Click on the "Add Fingerprint" button to launch the setup process.

4. When prompted, enter the password for your account.

5. Once authenticated, choose which finger you'd like to use with Touch ID and gently roll that finger over the Touch ID sensor. Make sure to gently roll over the sides and top and bottom of your finger, while lightly lifting your finger off and back onto the sensor as you watch the on-screen prompts to ensure that the sensor captures a complete sample.

6. Once it has successfully captured your fingerprint data, click the "Finish" button to return to the Touch ID preference pane.

7. A total of three fingerprints may be captured using three separate fingers. If you wish to add more, repeat steps 1–6 until all fingerprints are captured.

8. Last, under the Use Touch ID for section, make sure a checkmark is placed **only** next to the services you wish to keep protected with Touch ID.

   a. **Unlocking your Mac**: Authenticates and logs you onto your Mac.

   b. **Apple Pay**: Approves purchases made with Apple's payment platform – online and in-person.

   c. **iTunes Store, App Store, and Apple Books**: Makes media & content purchases using the stored financial data in Apple Wallet.

   d. **Password Autofill**: Automatically enters account information for websites saved with your credentials for easy login.

   e. **Use Touch ID sensor for fast user switching**: Permits additional users who also have Touch ID enabled within the same computer to quickly login without interrupting any other user's sessions.

Software Update

Apple, like any operating system developer, has a built-in system to search for and install updates for macOS. In fact, macOS boasts two software update capabilities: A GUI-based one, which is the one most users are familiar with, accessible by going to System Preferences | Software Update.

While there isn't much to configure here, the aim of updating software is to *perform* the updates on a regular cadence so that your Mac receives the latest protection from known threats and vulnerabilities.

It's easy for the average user to get bogged down when actually using their computer for work, school, or personal usage reasons that they totally lose sight of updates as they're released. That's ok because there are a few configurable settings available to make this a breeze. It can be set up so that macOS automatically takes care of the update process itself with as little user intervention as possible.

Configure Software Update settings (GUI)

1. Launch System Preferences | Software Update.

2. Click the "Advanced..." button to configure advanced settings.

3. A list of settings will be presented. Place a checkmark next to each setting you wish to have macOS automatically take care of for you:

    a. **Check for updates**: Checks for the existence of new updates regularly and makes users aware when new updates are available.

    b. **Download new updates when available**: Takes it one step forward from the previous and actually downloads new updates but does **not** install them.

    c. **Install macOS updates**: Takes it one step further still and actually installs only the updates pertaining to macOS versions, prompting users if/when a restart is required.

    d. **Install app updates from the App Store**: Downloads and installs application updates (not macOS updates) *only* for apps obtained from the Mac App Store.

e. **Install system data files and security updates**: Similar to preceding "C", this setting installs files needed by the system as well as security updates, which are different from the updates to a newer version of macOS, but arguably much more important.

The second software update capability is available through Terminal and requires administrator access to the Mac to accomplish. This is more aimed at IT professionals and administrators tasked with managing large fleets of Mac computers simply because it is far less user friendly than the GUI version described previously, plus anyone – regardless of experience level – can potentially cause serious harm to macOS, including data loss, if they enter the wrong command when using Terminal, so proceed at your own risk...you've been warned!

Configure Software Update settings (Terminal)

1. Launch Terminal.

2. Enter the following command to manually check for all available updates, install them, and reboot your Mac once installation is complete:

```
sudo softwareupdate -aiR
```

Within Terminal, the *softwareupdate* command allows for greater flexibility over the management and control of updates, including viewing a list of available updates, restricting which updates are installed, downloading full installer binaries for later deployment, and scheduling updates among other management capabilities.

If you're an IT professional, budding Mac administrator, or are simply curious to learn more about how your Mac works in relation to Terminal commands and automation through scripting, an excellent place to gain information on the command referenced earlier is by checking the manual pages, referred to as "man pages" for short, by entering the following command in Terminal and scrolling through the full documentation Apple provides regarding the *softwareupdate* command:

```
man softwareupdate
```

Third-Party Patches

Not to be confused with Software Update in the previous section, which pertains exclusively to updating macOS, system, and security updates and apps downloaded only from the Mac App Store.

This section deals with keeping third-party applications up-to-date that have been downloaded and installed from sources other than Apple and the Mac App Store, like a developer's website, a repository of apps stored on your company's server or corporate applications developed in-house by your organization.

While this section is a bit difficult to quantify due to the nature of third-party apps being, well, developed by third parties and therefore out of the scope of Mac's built-in updating tools. I'd never forgive myself for not even mentioning that all applications on your Mac – especially those not created by Apple – should be regularly updated too in order to keep Apple computers as secure as possible from threats while preserving user privacy.

How to go about doing this exactly varies from app to app, so if you're looking for some silver bullet solution to quickly and easily keep your third-party apps updated, I'm sorry to burst your bubble. At the consumer level, there's really only manually checking each of your apps regularly to ensure you're using the most recent version.

Thankfully many developers have implemented a simple "Check for updates…" mechanism within their apps that allows the app to check against the developer's servers for new updates. If updates are present, this mechanism will usually download the app and offer to install it as well. Other times, the update mechanism will alert the user that a new update is available, then provide them a link to where it can be manually downloaded and installed. It's not automated, but better than nothing.

For IT pros and Mac admins, there's a rather large silver lining to be seen here *if* your Macs are managed through an MDM solution. Let me explain, thanks to Apple's ESF, MDM solution providers have been provided blueprints in a sense that guide them to managing various aspects of macOS, one of these being third-party application deployments and by extension, updates to these apps.

Now, the actual deployment and updating of third-party apps will vary somewhat from one MDM solution to another. Furthermore, there's no way for me to possibly know which MDM solution you are using, nor the variables related to your organization's management infrastructure, taking it far from the scope of this book.

What I do know is that chances are great if you're using a modern MDM solution that adheres to Apple's security and privacy frameworks that contacting the developer or searching their website will provide access to support documentation that covers the deployment and update process in detail. Additionally, some MDM providers have even developed tools to assist (and some even automate) software management to such a degree that IT admins need only select which packages they wish to deploy and select which groups of devices they wish to deploy them to – the MDM takes care of the rest, including keeping supported third-party applications up-to-date.

File and Folder Permissions

This section is not for the faint of heart when it comes to macOS security. I'm not trying to scare or dissuade users from modifying file and folder permissions, but I am trying to underscore the importance of paying attention to what you're doing and knowing what each setting means *before* committing to it as it's entirely possible to lock yourself (or someone else) out of accessing their data, so please be careful when attempting any of what follows in this section.

For those that don't know or are unsure, every file and folder within macOS has a set of permissions tied to it. Depending on what the system, IT admin, or user is trying to achieve, each file and folder stored on your Apple computer will allow or deny access to the data, copying, reading, editing, or deleting – each of these actions are governed by a permission and what the permission is configured to allow the user to do. If a user isn't allowed to perform a specific action, it's simply not allowed and therefore denied, by default.

It's easy to see where modifying permissions could lead to a stronger, more protected Mac, while simultaneously giving the impression that something can go very wrong very quickly if incorrect permissions are set. Both summations are equally correct, hence why the disclaimer to be very careful before changing permissions.

First, we look at files since file permissions – while mostly identical to folder permissions – do vary slightly in the number of options available. For starters, file permissions only affect the file whose permissions are being modified – that's it. *One* set of permissions for *one* file directly impact **and** affect *just* the **one file**. Whereas with folder permissions, you can set permissions on a folder that will affect just the folder – not the files contained within that directory. Or, you can force the files stored within that directory to have the same permissions level as what was set on the folder, effectively overwriting the permissions originally set on the files.

Similar to the Software Update section where I covered the GUI and Terminal versions of performing that task, managing permissions is also made possible from both the GUI and Terminal, respectively.

Let's use an example to best describe how to change file and folder permissions using the GUI method. Assume you have a file stored on your Desktop called "MySecretFile.doc" and you don't want anyone but you to access it.

1. Right-click the file and select "Get Info" from the context menu to bring up the file properties.

2. Scroll down to the "Sharing & Permissions" section, then click the padlock icon on the bottom-right to authenticate.

3. After successfully unlocking the file, look at the box with the names of users and their respective privilege. Find your account name within the list (suffixed with "(Me)") and ensure your privilege level is "Read & Write."

4. Next, find the "Staff" group (of which each user account on that Mac is a member of, by default) and click on the name once to highlight it, then press the "-" to delete the group.

5. Since the "Everyone" group (which refers to any user on the Mac, including service accounts, etc.) cannot be deleted, their permission will need to be changed. Click on the privilege level next to the group's name and select "No Access" from the drop-down menu.

6. Close the file's property window and the settings will be saved for that file with the modified permissions. Now only you can access that file and no one else.

In the event that you're accessing a file on a Mac with multiple user accounts and security groups created, you simply need to repeat steps 4–5 for each account and user group type until your account is the last one available with "Read & Write" access. Any accounts/groups that cannot be deleted, should have the privilege level changed to "No Access" to restrict the file's access.

Remember when I mentioned earlier that setting folder permissions is mostly identical to file permissions except for a few options? Well, it's really just one option, and it's located at the very bottom of the folder properties box. If you click on the ellipsis next to the "+" and "-" buttons, a drop-down box reveals the "Apply to enclosed items…" option.

After making changes to a folder, if the user selects that option, they'll be prompted with a dialog box asking to verify if you wish to apply the selected permissions to all enclosed items. It also tells you this is something that cannot be undone. Clicking the "OK" button will force all the files and folders contained within that parent folder to have the same permissions set on them as the parent folder.

This is helpful if you need to set the same permission levels across a large group of files and subdirectories, but it's as dangerous as it is helpful if this option is selected when it shouldn't have been. By incorrectly modifying the permissions on affected files and folders, large security implications may have been created that need to be addressed immediately before unauthorized users are able to access sensitive data or equally, authorized users are locked out of data critical to their job role.

You might be thinking, that's not so difficult, why the cryptic warning earlier? You're right, this level of file permission is very basic and easy to accomplish. Most files, especially those that are contained within a user's home folder, are pre-configured, so the account owner also has Read & Write access to their data. This is done by macOS to maintain security and privacy between multiple user accounts within the same Mac. User A has access to their files while User B has access to their files, while A can't read B's files or vice versa.

The difficult part really gets amplified when it relates to files:

- Outside the home folder structure, like files shared by multiple users

- Files contained in directories (folders)

- Multiple sub-directories contained within parent directories

- Large numbers of users and security groups

- Large numbers of files and folders

What happens when each of these cases are introduced is that each variable requires a certain level of changes to be configured just right to ensure security without inadvertently giving any unauthorized user or group access they shouldn't have while ensuring that authorized users aren't blocked from accessing data they should have. It's a delicate balancing act that only grows exponentially more difficult as variables are combined.

For the second part of this section, the Terminal will be used to modify permissions on files and folders. There are two ways to perform this within macOS, named Symbolic Notation and Octal Notation. Both are performed through the Terminal using the *chmod* command and can be difficult to master, but the latter requires the utmost care to avoid creating a larger security issue due to miscalculation.

Symbolic Notation: Uses a series of attributes, defined as letters to add or remove permissions from users, groups, and/or world to files and folders.

Basically, the way it breaks down is this, there are three groupings that permissions are assigned to:

- **Owner**

- **Group**

- **World**

The permissions assigned to each grouping appear as letter attributes that appear as a line of ten characters (Ex. drwxr--r--)

In the preceding example, each character (even the dashes) represents a permission or lack thereof. Depending on the letter placement, a specific permission is granted to a specific grouping. Let's take a closer look at that example:

Symbolic Notation Permissions Example

Identifies if the referenced object is a folder, link or file	d	d = directory
		l = symbolic link
		- = file
Permissions set from characters 2-4 appy to the Owner.	r	r = can read
	w	w = can write
	x	x = can execute
Permissions set from characters 5-7 appy to the Group.	r	r = can read
	-	- = cannot write
	-	- = cannot execute
Permissions set from characters 8-10 appy to the World (Everyone).	r	r = can read
	-	- = cannot write
	-	- = cannot execute

Symbolic Notation Permissions Attributes

Refers to the file or directory owner	u
Refers to the group	g
Refers to the world, or others	o
Refers to all, or a combination of "u", "g" and "o"	a
Adds the selected permissions "r", "w", and/or "x" to the selected grouping	+
Removes the selected permissions "r", "w", and/or "x" from the selected grouping	-
Sets the selected permissions "r", "w", and/or "x" to the selected grouping, overwriting any previously existing permissions for the selected grouping	=

As you can see from the preceding chart, the referenced object is a directory (another name for folder) and the Owner of the folder has been granted permissions to read, write, and execute (or launch) the directory. The Group to which the owner belongs is only granted the read permission, as is the case with the World (or Everyone else). In the case of both group and world, the write and execute permissions are left empty, meaning they're both denied.

This translates to the owner of the directory having full rights to the folder, while anyone that is part of the group (except the owner) can only read the contents of the folder. Everyone else that isn't the owner or a member of the group, can only read the contents of the folder. So, how does this occur within Terminal? I'll show you next.

Setting permissions on a folder using Symbolic Notation

1. Launch Terminal.

2. Navigate to the location of the directory you wish to set permissions on. For the purposes of this tutorial, let's assume the directory named "Test1" is saved to the user's Desktop folder.

   ```
   cd ~/Desktop
   ```

   The *cd* command changes directories and the "~" refers to the logged-on user's home folder path, lastly "Desktop" is the name of the directory that we're changing to.

3. Once there, we'll use the chmod command to change the permissions on "Test1," followed by the string of attributes:

   ```
   chmod u+rwx,g-x,o-wx,g+r,o+r Test1
   ```

4. Upon successful execution, the owner of the directory will be granted read, write, and execute permissions, the group will be granted read and write permissions, while the others (world) will be granted only read permissions.

Note   The chmod command is flexible enough to work with multiple permission types across different groupings to add and remove permissions, as needed. It only requires the use of a "," to separate between permission types. Plus, it helps keep it organized at a glance.

Before moving on to Octal Notation, let me share a shortcut to obtain the permissions of a file or folder through Terminal. By using the *ls* command with the "-l" attribute, the command will list the contents of the current directory in the long format, which includes, among many other types of information, the security permissions set on each file and folder in the directory.

```
ls -l
```

```
ex. -rwxr--r--    1 username  staff       0 Aug 29 18:20 Test1
```

That was the easier part, Octal Notation represents a numerical take similar to symbolic notation, but this requires math to calculate permissions, which, for some, could be an order of magnitude more difficult to employ. But we'll work through it together!

Octal Notation: Uses a series of attributes, defined as numbers to add or remove permissions from users, groups and/or world to files and folders.

While permissions are still applied to the same three groupings previously identified, they appear as a three-digit number ranging from "000" to "777," depending on the specific permissions applied to the object. (Ex. 744)

In keeping with the same example as previously, the "Test1" directory, we can obtain the permissions set for that folder by using the *stat* command, followed by the attribute "-f" to designate a format. For the purposes of this tutorial, the format equivalent to octal notation output is "%0Lp."

```
stat -f "%0Lp"
```

```
ex. -rwxr--r-- 744 Test1
```

Octal Notation Permissions Meanings

Octal	Binary	Permission
0	000	---
1	001	--x
2	010	-w-
3	011	-wx
4	100	r--
5	101	r-x
6	110	rw-
7	111	rwx

The preceding chart has a breakdown of octal notation and its translation to binary and, more importantly, how it equates with symbolic notation.

The binary notation was included as it could come in handy down the road, but for the purposes of explaining file and folder permissions in this section, focus only on the octal numeral and its permission equivalent.

From the stat command output, we learned that the "Test1" directory has an octal permission of "744." Breaking that down further, the "7" references the Owner; "4" references the Group; and "4" references the World permission sets.

If you go back up to the symbolic section, you will note that the respective permissions were:

- Owner = rwx

- Group = r--

- World = r--

When you compare the octal and symbolic notations to the preceding permissions meanings chart, you'll see that they correlate perfectly.

- 7 = rwx

- 4 = r--

- 4 = r--

Setting permissions on a folder using Octal Notation

1. Launch Terminal.

2. Navigate to the location of the directory you wish to set permissions on. For the purposes of this tutorial, let's assume the directory named "Test1" is saved to the user's Desktop folder.

   ```
   cd ~/Desktop
   ```

3. Once there, we'll use the chmod command to change the permissions on "Test1," followed by the string of attributes:

   ```
   chmod 744 Test1
   ```

4. Upon successful execution, the owner of the directory will be granted read, write, and execute permissions, the group will be granted read and write permissions, while the others (world) will be granted only read permissions.

That's it! Octal notation, from a certain point of view, appears easier and it could very well be for users and IT admins that find it simpler than contending with symbolic notation's use of symbols and characters to add and subtract permissions. Use what you feel most comfortable with.

Before moving onto the next section, I'll just leave you with this regarding octal notation. It's math-based as mentioned before, so if you reference the preceding permission meanings chart, you'll see that read (r) = "4," write (w) = "2" and execute (x) = "1," right? If you set all three permissions to an object, that user, group, or world will get a "7," because 4 + 2 + 1 = ? You guessed it!

Note   For a variation on the stat command that outputs both symbolic and octal notation permissions of an object, use the following command:

```
stat -f "%Sp %OLp %N" Test1
ex. -rwxr--r-- 744 Test1
```

Sharing Preferences

The Sharing preference pane is where users and admins go to control access to the sharing of numerous resources that are contained within your Mac.

In fact, there are a total of eleven services that can be managed from here that enable or disable access to your Mac in different ways. By default, they are all disabled to maintain the security of Apple computers and should only be enabled *if* necessary. Furthermore, when enabled, each service should be hardened to keep Mac as safe as possible, even with one or more services enabled. It'll be more difficult, mind you, but it is possible to do so.

Let's look at the different services available, shall we?

1. **Screen sharing:** Allows users on other computers to view and control your computer remotely.

2. **File sharing:** Allows other users to access shared folders on your computer while administrators can access all volumes.

3. **Media sharing:** Devices on your network, like a Smart TV can browse and play music, movies and TV shows from your Mac. Also, media sharing between Apple devices and/or guests is possible.

4. **Printer sharing:** Allow network users to print to use the printer connected to your Mac over the network.

5. **Remote login:** Enables your account – and any accounts you designate – to login remotely to your computer using Secure Shell (SSH) and Secure File Transfer Protocol (SFTP).

6. **Remote management:** Different from the preceding remote login, this service allows designated users to access your computer remotely using Apple Remote Desktop (ARD) management software designed for IT admins, permitting them to manage multiple Apple devices from a single, remote management station.

7. **Remote Apple events:** This service permits other macOS-based computers to send their logging data, such as login history, errors, or other logs generated by Mac to your computer. This is done by IT to better manage the macOS devices they're responsible for by centralizing logging data.

8. **Internet sharing:** Share the Internet connection on your Mac with other devices, enabling your Mac to act as a gateway over Wi-Fi, Ethernet, or Thunderbolt-based adapters.

9. **Bluetooth sharing:** Allow your Mac to share files with other Bluetooth-enabled devices.

10. **Content caching:** This service configures your Mac as a central repository for content downloaded from Apple, specifically, software updates, apps, and purchases from the App, iTunes and Book Stores, respectively. This allows other Apple computers on the same network to obtain updates from your Mac instead of over the Internet, as is the default behavior saves bandwidth. Barring few exceptions, this service is mainly aimed at IT administrators and small-medium and large-sized organizations.

11. **AirPlay receiver:** This service allows other devices currently signed in with your Apple ID to see and share media content directly with your Mac.

As you can see from the list of services, some of these are straightforward in the functionality they offer and how they're managed, while others still could lead to complexity or lead to larger security issues if misconfigured.

Screen sharing: Unless you're a Mac admin and require this functionality, screen sharing should remain turned off. If it's truly necessary, a better solution is Remote Management and ARD since that offers greater security, but it does require purchasing the ARD software from the Mac App Store. Still, if you're set on using screen sharing, make sure to limit the users and groups that can access your Mac from the users' list. Also, by clicking on "Computer Settings...," check the box next to "VNC viewers may control screen with password" and set a complex password to prevent this feature from being abused. There is a limitation of eight characters for the password (VNC's limitation – not Apple's) and make sure to leave the "Anyone may request permissions to control screen" box unchecked, as this allows anonymous users to access **and** control your Mac remotely.

File sharing: Similar to file and folder permissions that provision access to resources for local users, sharing permissions provision access to resources for network users. Though data may be shared locally within the same system without ever having to travel across the network, the main reason to configure sharing properties for the folder are to grant users and groups that do not have local access to your Mac access to the resources they need or are requesting.

For the sake of this section and the larger purpose of this book – to secure your Mac – we'll look at sharing permissions for directories that are currently stored on your Apple computer, not on a network share or on a remote server. But do know that the location of the data factors is very little when configuring sharing permissions. The greater concern is to secure the data so that those that you wish to authorize to access the data can do so, while those that do not require access are prevented from doing so, ensuring least privilege access (see User Account Types section), which helps to maintain security and preserve privacy.

Before we get started, be aware that configuring share permissions is not the same as setting file and folder permissions. The former grants users and groups access to the folders, like granting a colleague from your department access to read and write to the folder that contains the spreadsheet files for a project you're both working on; the latter *actually* permits the user to read, write, and execute the spreadsheet files you're working together on. Think of it like allowing a friend that visits your house to help get the ingredients from your refrigerator and peel vegetables for dinner, except you – the host – are the only one cooking, you don't permit your guest to cook since you want them to relax and enjoy themselves. In this scenario, gathering the ingredients would be the sharing permissions, while cooking would be the file and folder permissions. Two separate processes that are joined in one common goal – you can't have one without the other – at least, not securely.

Oh, and one last thing to remember: sharing permissions only apply directly to folders – not to files. You can always place any number of files within folders, including nested folders for organization purposes, but ultimately, what you're sharing access to are directories, not the files themselves. And before you ask, because of this design, multiple folders can (and often will require) different sets of sharing permissions.

This can add to sharing permissions being somewhat tricky, but it's made a heck of a lot easier when permissions are granted to groups instead of individual users. This reduces the number of times sharing permissions must be modified, each time a new user is to be added. For personal devices, it's not too bad, but in corporate environments or those with many users necessitating varying levels of permissions, it can get overwhelming very fast, so managing sharing permissions by groups – also known as role-based management – can make short work of an otherwise complex and time-consuming task.

There are three ways to configure sharing permissions on directories. Two rely on the GUI and are far simpler for scenarios that require minimal permission sets and few folders.

Set sharing permissions from Finder

1. Navigate to the location of a folder you wish to share.

2. Click on the folder once to highlight it, then right-click it and select "Get Info" from the context menu.

3. Click the padlock on the bottom-right corner to enable editing the properties for the folder after authenticating.

4. Under the "General" section, check the box next to "Shared Folder."

Note   If the File Sharing service is not enabled on your Mac yet, you will be prompted to do so before continuing. Click on the "Enable" button and authenticate once more to turn on the sharing service.

---

5. Sharing is now enabled for the selected folder. However, don't forget you may need to customize the folder permissions like we did in the previous section. Use the "+" and "-" buttons to add/remove accounts and groups to suit your needs and use the drop-down menu next to each to select the appropriate privileges.

6. When customized, close the folder properties and both sharing and file permissions will be configured for the selected folder.

Set sharing permissions from System Preferences

1. Launch System Preferences and click on the Sharing preference pane.

2. If the preferences are greyed out, click on the padlock along the bottom-left corner and authenticate to allow editing.

3. By default, the File Sharing service is disabled. Check the box next to File Sharing to enable it.

Note   You'll see the grey dot will turn green, meaning the service is enabled and displays an IP address with the name of the sharing service alongside it. This is the network location where your shared folders will live. Keep in mind that anyone on your network segment with this path and the required file and folder permissions will be able to access your shared data.

---

4. Under Shared Folders: Use the "+" and "-" buttons to add/remove access to shared folders.

5. Under Users: Use the "+" and "-" buttons to add/
    remove access to users and groups, alongside
    setting their privilege levels from their respective
    drop-down menus.

Set sharing permissions from Terminal

1. Launch Terminal.

2. If you already have a folder to share, skip to the next
    step. If not, we'll need to create one using the *mkdir*
    command first by entering the following command:

    ```
    mkdir /Path/to/folder
    ```

3. With a folder ready, we now need to configure it for
    sharing using the –wait for it – *sharing* command.
    This will create a Small Message Block (SMB) share,
    which is compatible with all OS types. To do this,
    we will use the "-a" attribute to identify the path to
    the folder we're sharing, use the "-S" attribute to
    create a "name" for the share and finally, use the
    "-s" attribute (no that's not a typo, macOS Terminal
    commands **are** case-sensitive after all) to configure
    the share be enabled once the command completes.

    ```
    sudo sharing -a /Path/to/folder -S "Share_
    Name" -s 001
    ```

4. With the folder created and share enabled, our job
    is done, right? Wrong! This is about security, so we
    now need to configure the folder permissions using
    either the GUI or Terminal, using symbolic or octal
    notation (check the last section for a refresher on
    configuring file and folder permissions).

Media sharing: If you do not plan to share media, then keep this service turned off. However, if you plan to do so, start by checking the box to enable this service. Next to "Library Name," give it a unique name. Home Sharing is a service extension tied into your Apple ID that shares the library across all devices with your Apple ID currently signed in. If this is something you'd like, check the box next to Home Sharing to establish that link. Lastly, sharing with guests is disabled by default. Though if you wish to enable that, simply check the box next to "Share media with guests" and click the "Options…" button to further drill-down what types of media will be shared, as well as configuring a password before guests can access media content by checking the box next to "Require Password" and entering a strong password to secure access.

Printer sharing: If it's not necessary, please keep this service disabled. If required, check the box to enable this service and you'll see a list of the printers connected locally to your mac under the Printers section. This only applies to those connected via cable directly – network or AirPrint-enabled devices cannot be shared from here. Click on the printer you wish to share and use the "+" and "-" buttons to add/remove accounts under the Users section to grant/deny sharing access.

Remote login: Be very careful with this service. It really only serves the purpose if A) you **need** to access devices remotely; B) you're proficient with the Terminal; C) you (or anyone you're designating access to) are confident you (and/or they) won't nuke your computer in the process. If you answered "YES" to each of these instances and are fully aware of the risk, then check the box to enable this service. Under "Allow access for," select the radio button next to "Only these users" – never "All Users" – and use the "+" and "-" buttons to add/remove accounts that will remotely access your computer through SSH and SFTP. Last, and this one is critical too – do not check the box next to "Allow full disk access for remote users" unless you're 100% certain you or the user(s) you're designating require it. If something goes wrong, like a fumbled command or if the account becomes compromised, it could lead to catastrophic failure of your Mac, including granting a bad actor unfettered access to every corner of macOS.

Bear in mind the Peter Parker principle popularized in Spider-Man comic books written by Stan Lee, "*With great power comes great responsibility.*"

Remote management: File this under the "if you don't need it, don't enable it section" as well. If you do require it, check the box to enable the service and under the "Allow access for" section, select the radio button next to "Only these users" and use the "+" and "-" buttons to add/remove accounts that will have access to manage your Mac remotely. This includes modifying configurations, changing settings…basically, nothing short of having full administrator access to Mac. Like screen sharing, but with better security, clicking the "Computer Settings…" button allows you to check the box next to "VNC viewers may control screen with password" and then set a strong password. Leave the "Anyone may request permission to control screen" checkbox disabled and check the "Always show Remote Management status in menu bar" box, which displays management status in the Menu Bar. Last, yet extremely important, click the "Options…" box to display a list of permissions that are possible with ARD. Check only the boxes that you require, leave the rest unchecked to limit unapproved access to your Mac.

Remote Apple events: This is largely an IT and Mac admin function so chances are rather high that personal users will not need this and should therefore leave this disabled. Administrators know the drill by now, check the box to enable the service and "+" and "-" buttons to add/remove accounts that will have access.

Internet sharing: If you ever find yourself needing to share internet access with other devices, this is a useful feature to enable only during use. The rest of the time, it is an unnecessary risk and should be disabled. Check the box to enable it when needed, selecting your Mac's internal connection that you'll be sharing (Wi-Fi and Ethernet, for example).

Next, in the "To Computers using" section, check the box next to the ports you'll be sharing to (Ethernet, Thunderbolt, and/or Wi-Fi). If selecting Wi-Fi, additional settings will need to be configured by clicking the "Wi-Fi Options…" button, where you can set the temporary wireless network's name, settings, and password that users of other devices can use to share your internet access. Remember, when it's no longer needed, turn the service off.

Bluetooth sharing: Similar to the preceding, if you don't need it, don't enable it. If you do find yourself in need of it, it's handy to share files with other devices wirelessly. This one we're going to configure backwards due to the potential for security abuse. If you're not going to receive items, set it to "Never Allow" from the drop-down menu next to "When receiving items," this prevents any device from sending you files you didn't request. Same thing applies to "When other devices browse," if you're not sharing anything with anyone, set it to "Never Allow." However, sharing is about sending and receiving data, so if you need to do either, select the most restrictive option "Ask what to do." This leaves your Mac open to establishing connections with Bluetooth-enabled devices, but it doesn't complete the connection until you authorize the transmission to occur, giving you a chance to review what's being sent and/or received **before** it's sent or saved to your Mac. When the settings are configured, then we check the box to enable the service. Oh, and don't forget, you may need to click the "Open Bluetooth Preferences…" button to *first* establish a paired connection with other devices before data can be shared.

Content caching: Like the preceding Remote Apple Events, this is a predominantly IT and Mac admin feature that offers personal users little to no benefit, instead, it actually impacts performance by using your bandwidth to download updates for Apple and eats up storage space by saving it to your Mac's storage drive. If it's something you wish to take advantage of as an administrator, first select the content type you wish to store next to Cache. Leaving it as "All Content" isn't a problem since Apple's tuned this service for efficiency, but if you only need to cache updates, selecting "Shared Content" limits what's downloaded and stored to just that content type. Next, click on the "Options..." button which displays a sliding scale used to set how much storage space will be used by the caching service. By default, it's supposed to leave approximately 20% as reserves for macOS to function properly, but if you're using your Mac for other storage-intensive tasks, you could find yourself running out of space rather quickly, so adjust it to what you estimate you'll need. Worst case scenario? If you need more space, simply adjust the scale to gain more space on-the-fly. Last, check the box to enable the service but note, it can sometimes take about ten to fifteen minutes to register with Apple and start to serve updates across your local network.

AirPlay receiver: This service really only ties into streaming content from one Apple device to your Mac or from your Mac to another device. As far as security is concerned, it's rather low compared to the other services on this list. But that doesn't mean it should be ignored. If you're not using it, disable it. If you do use it, a good way to limit risk is to select the "Current User" radio button under the "Allow AirPlay for" section. This keeps access to your account only – no one else. For added security, check the box next to "Require password" and enter a complex password to enhance security should someone gain access to a device of yours that currently has your Apple ID logged in. This prevents unauthorized users from streaming anything to/from your Mac without entering the password first.

System Integrity Protection (SIP)

macOS has a built-in technology that protects the entire system from the execution of unauthorized code called SIP. By default, it is enabled and remains enabled until an administrator explicitly disables it.

As stated, its primary function is to prevent unauthorized code from running on your Mac.[19] For the purposes of this book, unauthorized code in this context means any such application, system drivers, or extensions that are attempted to be launched or installed that are not downloaded from the Mac App Store or notarized by developers registered with Apple.

In essence, System Integrity Protection exists to enforce code signed through notarization, as well as preventing low-level code, such as that of drivers that interface with hardware, like printer software or when adding additional ports to your Apple computer.

Because of this technology's ability to effectively block malicious and otherwise unwanted code, it can sometimes interfere with the app testing phase when developing in-house apps and services for macOS. Apple has provided a means for administrators to temporarily disable SIP – if and when necessary – to allow app testing to occur unaffected by the limitations imposed by SIP.

Note   While it is not advisable to disable SIP, should the need arise, it is possible. Best security practices dictate that SIP should be reenabled when testing is completed to avoid leaving Mac vulnerable to executing malicious code.

Extensions

We're familiar with apps. Bundles of software code that empower users to accomplish tasks in relation to managing and manipulating data. Extensions for macOS and Safari are just that, mini bundles of code that

---

[19] https://developer.apple.com/documentation/security/disabling_and_enabling_system_integrity_protection

offer users the ability to customize the way macOS and Safari works. It achieves this by installing within macOS or Safari, where the extension is designed to add greater capabilities to either.

Like any such app, extensions can also be weaponized in a manner to take advantage of flaws in macOS security, introduce them, or bypass them altogether. It is for this very reason that users should be very careful when installing extensions to either macOS or Safari[20] – even from somewhere as secure as the Mac App Store – to ensure that access to sensitive data is minimized while user privacy is upheld.

After all, even legitimate apps free from malicious code could gain access to data that users may not wish for them to have. For example, Safari is used to access websites online. An extension to Safari, such as a search add-on to help find websites more relevant to your search requires collecting search terms and the URL of websites accessed…maybe even browsing history. Assuming this extension is not compromised or acting in any way suspicious, the sheer fact that it has access to your browsing habits and history may be enough to warrant not using this type of extension at all.

Luckily, Apple has implemented a simple yet effective way of checking for and denying access to extensions that have been installed either directly or indirectly on macOS and Safari.

Manage extensions in macOS

1. Launch System Preferences, then click on the Extensions preference pane.

2. On the left will be a list of categories, clicking on each will expand the list of app extensions installed on your Mac along with what rights they've been granted using the familiar checkbox system.

---

[20] https://support.apple.com/guide/safari/get-extensions-sfri32508/mac

3. Since everyone's experience could potentially
    be different, it's considered a good practice to
    regularly review each category and manually disable
    any extensions or access permissions granted to
    extensions to minimize risk of data loss or theft.

Manage extensions in Safari

1. Launch Safari, then click on Safari | Preferences...
    from the Menu Bar.

2. Click on Extensions from the properties menu to
    view the list of extensions installed within Safari,
    including getting a description of what they do, the
    permissions allocated to them, and an Uninstall
    button to remove them altogether.

3. Like extensions in macOS, they provide a checkbox
    system to disable/enable the extension. And the
    aforementioned Uninstall button performs a
    complete removal of the extension from Safari,
    should that be necessary.

Time Machine

Backups, the time-honored tradition that offers users the ability to save
their data by storing it on a secondary storage medium so that, in the event
of a disaster, users can prevent (or at least significantly limit) data loss
by restoring the data lost on one medium with the duplicate created and
stored on the second medium.

Pardon me if that line sounds a little disingenuous. It's not, I swear! But
it is tinged with a hint of sarcasm only – not because backing up data isn't a
valid solution – no, it totally is. No, the hint stems primarily from users not
taking advantage of it and secondarily from the excuses that users provide
for not doing so.

Eye Roll aside, I consider myself a "glass half full" kind of IT person, so here, in this book, we're going to focus on all the benefits to back-up your data regularly, including strategies to do so efficiently, securely, and, most importantly, easily, with the help of Apple's backup solution called Time Machine.

First, Time Machine is included in every modern version of macOS, and it's baked right in, meaning it's free and doesn't cost users one cent to implement it. Second, Time Machine was designed with Apple's approach of taking even the most complex, technical processes and boiling them down to a simple-to-use-yet-powerful process that can benefit all Apple computer users.

Time Machine automatically keeps regularly scheduled backups of your data in the following ways:

- Local snapshots as space permits

- Hourly backups for the past 24 hours

- Daily backups for the past month

- Weekly backups for all the previous months

It does this on at least one storage disk, though it can handle multiple disks to ensure that data is copied to several different locations for failover purposes. Lastly, as a disk becomes full, the oldest backups contained within that disk are deleted to make room for newer snapshots without risk of data loss due to incrementally backing up data over days, weeks, months, and years.

Note   The only requirement to use Time Machine is at least one storage disk to copy data to. Whether it be a locally connected disk, like a USB Drive, Network-based disk, like a NAS or one connected to your router.

Setup Time Machine to back-up your Mac

1. Launch System Preferences, then click on the Time Machine preference pane.

2. Click the "Select Backup Disk..." button to bring up a list of the disks connected to your Mac over wired or wirelessly. Click once to highlight the disk you wish to use, then click the "Use Disk" button.

Note   If you wish to enable encryption – and this being a security-focused book, you should for added protection. Check the box next to "Encrypt backups" prior to clicking the "Use Disk" button.

---

3. By default, Time Machine is configured to back-up the select system files but more importantly, the entire home directory for the locally logged-in account. If you wish to modify this by adding certain directories or individual files to be excluded from the backup, click the "Options..." button, then the "+" to bring up Finder. Navigate to the file(s) and/or folder(s) you wish to exclude, then click the "Exclude" button. Finally, click the "Save" button to commit the changes.

4. Last thing, if you wish to automate Time Machine, meaning it will create a system-based reminder for macOS to back-up your data regularly without user intervention, check the "Back Up Automatically" box on the main Time Machine preference pane and the service will start backing up your data immediately from that point onward.

Remote Wipe

If you've been an Apple user for some time, particularly an iPhone, you may be familiar with the iCloud service, Find My iPhone, that helps users to, well, find their iPhones in case they've been lost or stolen. Several years ago, Apple expanded this service to include macOS, bringing users the same capability to locate their macOS device, including the "Play Sound" feature which plays an audible noise to help you find your Apple device, say under the couch.

But that's not all, the iCloud service also permits users to "Lock" their device, by sending a remote signal to macOS that effectively locks the screen and won't allow it to be unlocked until the lock command is canceled or the user physically logs onto their Mac with their Apple ID. This feature is incredibly handy in the event of a device being lost or stolen, as it prevents unauthorized users from accessing the data stored on the device. But sadly, that isn't always enough to keep data safe.

The last feature and the star of this section is a bit of a double-edged sword for some to handle since it is the "Erase Mac" setting, a feature that – once sent – remotely communicates to your Mac a command that immediately gets processed, resulting in the Mac formatting or erasing all its contents. The process eradicates all traces of data from the Mac and along with it, any chance of recovering your Mac from loss or theft.

Like I said, it isn't something everyone will be too keen on, given the prospect of potentially forever losing your coveted Mac. But the flipside – and one that many organizations feel is a worthwhile trade off – is that the ability to ensure that data is erased from the Mac's drive means that even if bad actors got ahold of the device, any sensitive and/or critical data would be destroyed *before* they can get to it and more importantly, **before** any significant damage stemming from data breaches to violating regulatory compliance or leaking of company secrets can occur.

This should be considered a "last ditch" effort, but one that will work as long as the device in question is accessible from the internet.

Send erase Mac command from iCloud

1. Login to iCloud.com from any computer and authenticate.

2. Click on "Find My iPhone," then find the "dot" on the map that represents your missing device. Click on it to bring up the options.

3. To send the remote wipe command, click on "Erase Mac" once. You will be prompted to confirm the command. Click the "Erase" button once more to verify and the command will be sent.

4. Once the Mac is online, it takes only a few minutes to process the command and immediately following that, the formatting process begins. On Apple computers with Secure Enclave, the process occurs instantly; otherwise it takes approximately ten to fifteen minutes to complete on Intel Macs. Once it's done, the Mac will be wiped and at the initial Setup screen (like the first time it was ever powered on) all data will be gone.

Send the erase Mac command from Find My app

1. Launch Applications | Find My.app.

2. After a few minutes, the status of your Mac will update on the map. Click on the "Mac" icon that represents your device to bring up the options.

3. To send the remote wipe command, click on "Erase This Device" once. You will be prompted to confirm the command. Click the "Continue" button once more to verify and the command will be sent.

4. Once the Mac is online, it takes only a few minutes to process the command and immediately following that, the formatting process begins. On Apple computers with Secure Enclave, the process occurs instantly; otherwise It takes approximately ten to fifteen minutes to complete on Intel Macs. Once it's done, the Mac will be wiped and at the initial Setup screen (like the first time it was ever powered on) all data will be gone.

Summary

In this chapter, we dove into the internal protections of macOS against external vectors and how configuring them with security in mind minimizes the potential risk they present for threats to succeed.

We also provided in-depth explanations of concepts, like file permissions and provided step-by-step instructions where possible on how to configure your Mac computer to safeguard it and private data against a multitude of external threats.

Additionally, multiple ways of implementing protections were provided to give personal users as well as IT and Mac admins new to Apple an advantage when looking for the most flexible way of keeping Mac safe. Lastly, we also covered ways to avoid or minimize the risk associated with combined threats, discussing steps, considerations, and best practice recommendations to take advantage of the myriad tools and software technologies alongside your Mac to further minimize risk and exposure.

PART III

The Spoon Does Not Bend – Only Yourself

For the final two chapters of this book, we turn away from the hands-on approach and tutorials aimed at new users to Apple security. Instead, these next sections in the finale of the book are more geared to IT professionals and Mac admins. In Part III of this book, we pivot somewhat – still on trajectory with securing Mac – however, slightly repositioning the view toward the future of Mac management, by focusing on the types of enterprise technologies currently available and coming down the pike that add value to IT management and security workflows relating to Apple computers, including managed app deployment, automation, and designing a defense in-depth plan that benefits your organization and aligns itself and enforces company security and compliance policies.

CHAPTER 9

Work Smarter, Not Harder

During my IT career, I've met a wide range of individuals with varying levels of experience, expertise, and professionalism. Adding complexity to this are the multitude of different job roles and the tasks I've been responsible for completing – both as an individual contributor as well as in a group setting.

One concept that I developed early on that has served me well while acting as a driver that continues to help me seek out, obtain, and refine my skills while adding to my knowledge base is that of, "work smarter, *not* harder."

I apply that to everything I do and, whenever possible, try my best to abide by this saying. It doesn't mean "don't work hard" or "do the minimum" – nope. It simply refers to working hard when you need to – but the rest of the time, better the processes, workflows, support, and contributions you make to a task or project – regardless of how large or small – so that by evolving yourself through your updated tasks, you won't *always* have to work so hard.

What do you do with the time saved by not needing to work so hard? Take a vacation, you deserve it! But after you've recharged your batteries so to speak, reinvest some of that time saved into yourself by iteratively

© Jesus Vigo, Jr. 2023
J. Vigo, Jr., *Hardening Your Macs*, https://doi.org/10.1007/978-1-4842-8939-6_9

seeking out new opportunities to overcome challenges that will work to further boost your skills and knowledge base, making you far more versatile and effective as an IT professional and/or Mac admin.

Remote Controlling Your Fleet

In Chapter 8, under Sharing Preferences, we discussed the built-in technologies Apple includes with macOS that allows users to control a Mac remotely over the same network. Though this feature allows Mac to be controlled across other networks, that bit requires an additional third-party component to be installed and possibly additional configuration of the network devices that connect a user on a Mac sitting in one network to communicate and remotely control another Mac sitting on a different network. This delves into more advanced IT and Network administration processes that are beyond the scope outlined in this book.

However, for those that are seeking how to enable screen sharing and remote control, please revisit the Sharing section in the previous chapter for the full step-by-step instructions on enabling and securing this feature.

In this section, we're going to dive into some of the benefits of being able to control Mac remotely, as well as some of the different ways in which this is possible using the tools baked-in to macOS.

Screen sharing: Predominantly designed to share the screen on your Mac with authorized users and nothing more. This feature allows a remote user to see another's screen, just as if they were sitting directly at the computer themselves. This is intended to work in more of an assistive capacity, permitting a user to show another how something is done or to perform a function for a group demonstration. It's based on the Virtual Network Computing (VNC) standard, which is open source and, by default, insecure. The only protection available in its default configuration is an optional eight-character password that limits access to anyone without the password.

The VNC software has been modified by other third-party developers to include additional security components, such as Directory authentication support, advanced encryption, and newer security protocols, such as tunneling VNC connections through SSH for increased security. In many cases, these VNC alternatives are not free nor are they a part of Apple's built-in screen sharing bundle.

Apple remote desktop (ARD): Apple's first-party GUI-wrapper for its built-in screen sharing bundle provides many of the security enhancements of its third-party competitors, while incorporating remote management functionality native to macOS, allowing IT and Mac admins the ability to remotely manage Mac fleets in a one-to-many design. Many an administrator working remotely from their one Mac can establish a connection to all the Mac computers within their network that are configured for management.

While there are some technological advances that have occurred through the years that address and facilitate greater management capability over all Apple devices, not just macOS, making ARD slightly less desirable or flexible a solution as it once was. The fact remains that ARD can still provide administrators a great deal of management capability and flexibility when deploying applications, making changes to settings and providing an excellent one-to-one help desk tool for resolving client requests from users experiencing trouble with their Mac – by only lifting a finger.

Remote login: An excellent, Terminal-based option for administrators that are fluent and feel comfortable behind the keyboard using commands and scripting languages to manage Macs remotely. It's certainly not designed with user friendliness in mind, in fact, no terminal or command line prompts are known for this.

However, what they lack in user friendliness, they more than make up for in versatility, flexibility, speed, and most important for some, power. The Terminal, in expert hands, is capable of performing seemingly any task. Including combining multiple tasks in a chain to great effect. From configuring file and folder permissions to creating user accounts and groups to obtaining a litany of device health data and exporting it to customized reports for review later...again, there isn't much that cannot be done from the Terminal in capable hands.

Therein lies the duality of the Terminal and by extension, all remote-control software. In "not so capable" hands, it has the power to render macOS null, subject to data destruction, temporarily losing use of your Mac, and/or thoroughly impacting the user's experience for the worse.

Hollywood and the media often feature flashy scenes of users sitting in dark rooms with hoodies on. Madly mashing away at a keyboard, with each keystroke equating to a destructive sequence that renders a user's computer inoperable. This imagery isn't too far removed from the truth (sometimes). But what's left out is that, at times, even users with rudimentary knowledge at best can potentially cause similar levels of damage unknowingly, just because they didn't take heed as to the destructive potential their lack of knowledge could wreak. Hence why, regardless of your skill level, security is of paramount importance in macOS – whether it's protecting your Mac from outside threats, internal ones, or merely yourself.

Mobile Device Management (MDM)

MDM software are device management solutions that provide modern day capabilities, protection, and scale to meet the demands of your organization. While on-premises versions exist that are implemented and managed by your IT department, cloud-based solutions are more common, relying on the developer to spin-up virtual servers that support this software, making it accessible from anywhere in the world with an Internet connection for a monthly, per-device subscription fee.

There are many of these solutions available in the wild, some provide varying levels of support for multiple operating systems, while others still focus on just Apple devices, such as macOS- and iOS-based mobile devices. I won't go into the various solutions or recommend a specific one here, but I will discuss a few points that Mac admins should be aware of when selecting an MDM solution that could make the difference between addressing all your organizational concerns or failing to meet critical marks because of missing, underdeveloped, or simply unsupported features.

- **Infrastructure:** As mentioned, a majority of MDM solution providers are cloud-based. Though your organization may have the need to manage all services in-house, cloud based MDMs are preferred due to the developer managing and maintaining the hardware and network resources necessary to keep services up over 99% of the time. Furthermore, the always-accessible nature of cloud-based MDM solutions means devices are constantly checking-in with the service to update device records with relevant, useful information. Also, they're accessible from anywhere, at any time, and over any Internet-based connection which is critical to ensuring devices are managed with up-to-date patches, adhere to compliance policies, and are configured for maximum protection, among a range of other holistic benefits.

- **Same Day Support:** Apple releases new updates in a relatively frequent cadence. Not all updates offer new features for macOS, with some being tailored to patching a vulnerability or identified threat. One thing is certain, regardless of the reason, type or significance of an update, administrators are aware of how crucial it is to test and deploy updates as quickly after release as possible. Not all MDM solutions are built the same, and thus, it's critical to security and privacy efforts that organizations choose a solution that does offer same day support so that deployment plans are not delayed or prevented outright due to a lack of support by the developer.

- **Integration:** Not every organization has the same needs or requirements when it comes to their security strategies. This is normal and ultimately, administrators must do what they can within the parameters of their organizational requirements. Flexibility by extending solution capabilities is immensely useful to administrators by leveraging existing data from say an endpoint security solution that shares this data with your MDM to perform automated device remediation or installation of missing patches on macOS devices found to be out of compliance. Put another way, it's better to have integration capabilities and not need them, than need them and not have the ability to rely on them.

- **Apple Business Manager/Apple School Manager (ABM/ASM):** Technically an integration, I've decided to include this as a separate bullet point since it's not required of MDMs to support this nor are ABM/ASM required to use an MDM – but it makes Mac admins' life **so** much easier to use them in tandem. While we'll dive into this more later in the Zero Touch section, for now know that this is an Apple service that provides administrators a web-portal to aid in deploying macOS and iOS-based devices throughout their organization.

- **Alignment with Apple frameworks:** The topic of frameworks is another item we'll dive deeper into later in Chapter 10. But for now, know that Apple has designed frameworks which are software-based blueprints that enable functionality and provide developers, like MDM solution providers, with guidance on how to best secure Apple devices and uphold user privacy for users of Apple devices managed by MDM. Think of this as hiring a contractor to build your home; however, they're just going to "wing it" instead of building and ensuring a solid foundation first.

Device Configuration

macOS offers excellent security protections right out of the box. No one is disputing that. But if you're thinking that's the end of security or that your device is "perfectly secured against threats as is," I and thousands of security professionals around the world, including multiple government agencies, respectfully disagree with that notion. Not just for macOS, but for any computing device really.

The fact is that often, most computers are shipped from the factory with the latest version of its operating system available at the time. However, between the time the device is shipped and you power it on for the first time, any amount of time may have potentially passed, leaving the device outdated and therefore, vulnerable.

Not to mention the entirety of Chapters 7 and 8 of this book that speak directly to a whole host of security features and configurations that are, by default, not enabled. Hence why device configuration adds a critical element to securing your Mac.

Settings that are configurable within macOS exist throughout the operating system and affect any number of services, applications, and functionality either directly or indirectly. It's difficult to list every single setting that may be configured while also listing out every possible configuration since the combinations are vast and may change with each newer release of macOS and the evolution of the threat landscape for Apple-focused threats.

Moreover, I don't need to, as it's already been done and available in an easy-to-use application developed by Apple called Apple Configurator 2.[1] This software is free and hosted within the Mac App Store, providing a similar menu system to performing device configurations as MDM solutions use, thanks to its support of Apple's security frameworks.

It's a wonderful tool to get Apple users and administrators new to Mac management familiar with the ins and outs of Apple security, what are the different options available to configure and exactly how they can be configured. Also, it's easy to use and an informative GUI provides administrators detailed information pertaining to each setting and what their respective configurations mean for the security and privacy of your Mac – and the Macs you're tasked with managing.

Lastly, configurations can be exported as .mobileconfig files, which are binary bundles that contain XML-based data structures that contain payload information to configure the setting to the desired level, simply by launching the file and installing it.

After the first .mobileconfig file has been installed on macOS, a new preference pane called "Profiles" will appear within System Preferences. From here, users and admins alike can view all the configurations that have been installed, what they do and should the config be installed on an unsupervised device, the ability to remove a configuration will also be present. On supervised devices, those managed by a corporate MDM

---

[1] https://support.apple.com/apple-configurator

solution allow administrators to configure profiles as unremovable so as to prevent loss of function or weakened security due to a bad actor, threat, or malicious user removing the profile without authorization.

App Deployment

macOS has some of the simplest methods to install apps compared to its competitors. Apps, or packages as their sometimes referred to, come in three flavors:

- Bundle (.app)
- Flat Package (.pkg)
- Meta Package (.mpkg)

The bundle is the most common app and it only requires that user's drag the .app file to the Applications folder to install. Once the copy process is complete, the app is ready for use.

Flat packages are a bit more complicated, but not by much. The dependent files are compressed into the pkg format and users install these applications by either double-clicking them or opening them through the Installer. These usually require copying more files to various locations within macOS and often display wizards or windows that walk the user through the process, including progress bars that fill up as the installation process nears completion.

Meta packages are similar to flat packages, except they often contain more logic included which guides Installer through the process of installation. Typically, this logic checks for and ensures that any dependencies or pre-requisite software and tools are available before actually installing the application(s) contained within the meta package. It is often used when installing software suites that include more than one application.

One user deploying one app on one device is a trivial matter. Where it gets complicated is installing multiple apps on one device by one user. And yet more complicated still is one user installing many applications on many devices across multiple locations. This is where the power of technologies like ABM/ASM and MDM solutions really shine. ARD makes short work of installing apps to multiple devices from one management computer, but even still, it would prove several times more challenging to a Mac admin than relying on modern deployment structures that leverage cloud-based infrastructure, always-on network connections, device management frameworks, and automated workflows to make sure the apps users need are installed on their Mac when they need them – as opposed to when IT can get around to fulfilling the request on their help desk ticket.

Securing Devices

Apple's built-in security tools and frameworks offer great ways to protect a Mac from known threats. But is it enough? At the risk of saying yes or no definitively, the best answer is "it wholly depends on what you use your Mac for and how you go about doing it."

I know it seems like a "non-answer" but it really isn't when you stop to consider that, just like users use Mac for a variety of different reasons, organizations have a variable list of requirements, policies, and regulations that they must adhere to that is unique to their operating needs.

A bad answer would be to assume that each organization and user will use Mac in the same form and fashion. While it could be argued that this being the way, security would get a whole lot easier to implement since every Mac device would be used in the same way, with the same apps, each time by every user globally. But alas, this is a pipe dream, and in the real world, computing is every bit as much a form of self-expression as different hair styles or the clothes we choose to wear.

So, bearing this in mind, there are a number of built-in and third-party solutions that may be adopted by users and organizations alike to further secure macOS based on their unique needs and requirements. We covered the first-party ones earlier in this book, so in this section, we're going to touch upon the types of third-party endpoint security technologies that exist to mitigate risk and thwart a variety of Apple-focused threats. These protections are:

Malware: Signature- and behavioral-based technology that monitors, detects, removes, quarantines, and remediates against known malware-based threats.

Identity provision: Technology that leverages cloud-based identity providers, enabling centralized accounts to login and access macOS resources.

Remote access: Secure access to resources through policy-based, context-aware security paradigms (like Zero Trust) that prevent unauthorized access to compromised accounts or devices that do not meet the minimum requirements.

Centralized reports: Streaming of logging data to a centralized repository that collects, stores, and analyzes device telemetry data and alerts administrators in real-time to issues detected.

Content filter: Filtering technology that prevents access to websites that are known to be compromised, used in phishing campaigns and/ or blocked by organizations as necessary means to ensure business continuity isn't affected by threats to productivity.

Network-based: Securing communications over insecure networks, by leveraging encryption to ensure that data in motion stays protected from eavesdropping or MitM attacks.

Configuration management: MDM solutions fit this entry perfectly, with their ability to ensure that Apple devices are configured in accordance with best security practices and that software remains up-to-date.

Compliance enforcement: Technologies that fall into compliance enforcement aren't new, but not as widely known as MDM, for example. These tend to focus on keeping devices and their data secured by meeting a minimum baseline. Should devices fall below the baseline, policy-based software monitors and remediates the action. For example, Data Loss Prevention (DLP) software that monitors device use and actively prevents users from saving confidential data to unencrypted USB drives. If an unencrypted drive is detected, the software requires it to be encrypted *before* data will be permitted to be saved to that location.

Threat hunting: Another uncommon technology that is gaining traction among Security teams permits security professionals to monitor devices, gather suspicious data, and drill down more deeply into macOS to determine *if* a potentially unknown threat exists before it has a chance to grow into something far worse, like compromising your Mac or leading to a data breach.

Automating Workflows

The ability to automate workflows for IT and Mac admins strikes at the heart of the "work smarter, not harder" mantra. Though it's not possible to automate everything all the time due to the dynamic nature of technology and security, you can get close enough so that manually tedious tasks are handled automatically, freeing you up to work on more difficult challenges that do require your personal attention to resolve or complete.

Some software technologies offer this as a feature, like the aforementioned integration feature found in some MDM solutions. The ability to share threat data from one solution (security) directly with a second solution (management) creates the opportunity for administrators to configure the MDM solution to create security groups that place device records in one bucket that, for example, may have a specific app installed that is known to have a particular vulnerability that allows bad actors to take control with minimal effort.

Following on from this, a policy could be created that checks this security group every hour to determine which devices need to be updated. As the policy executes, all devices matching the criteria are automatically sent a command that deploys the latest version of the affected app – one with this vulnerability patched by the developer – to remedy the issue, resolving the critical finding without the user being impacted nor IT having to physically bring the device in for remediation.

While some automations may work like that, not all will. In fact, one of the simplest ways to get started automating on macOS is through the Terminal. More specifically, learning about how commands work, what they do, and how to perform them within Bash scripts. Bash being short for Bourne Again Shell, requires minimal investment beyond researching and experimenting in a closed environment (i.e., not production) to develop and test your skills at learning the Bash programming language and how it can be leveraged to perform nearly any management task(s) you can dream up.

It may not be easy at first, but as you get more experience and comfortable with Terminal – not to mention a little friendly advice from more experienced Mac admins always helps – you'll find yourself able to create full scripts that automate large tasks with ease. Better still, the more robust MDM solutions offer the ability to import your scripts for use in managing your macOS fleet should your organization choose to upgrade to a more modern and efficient method of management.

Zero Touch

Like automation, zero touch also embodies the spirit of my mantra. I must admit that upon initially learning of zero touch as an administrator at a large school, I was hesitant to embrace the technology. While I understood what it did and certainly saw the upside to it, there was this darker thought gnawing at me: how could I trust thousands of users to "do the right thing" when setting up their own Mac?

It is less about being unwilling to embrace new technology and more about not being able to clearly see how this technology could benefit *my* particular situation within the organization I was employed at.

I have come to love this technology, welcoming it with open arms and – dare I say it – they're probably my favorite two words in Mac management just after automation.

So, what *is* zero touch? Zero touch is a device management model that blends Apple Business Manager[2] (or Apple School Manager,[3] if you're in the education sector) and MDM to supervise, deploy, and manage company-owned Macs before they're delivered to employees.

Let me explain that last part. What I mean by "before they're delivered to employees" is that all these configurations and management settings are preset on the device before the device is even delivered. This means that when a device arrives, brand new and still sealed, it goes straight to the employee or user it's assigned to. They unbox it and power it on for the first time and, like magic, voilà! their device is ready to go and configured just for them from day one.

No manual intervention by IT. No requiring IT to do all the heavy lifting to customize the device for the role of the user, installing their software, blah, blah, blah. None of that is required.

Simply put:

1. Employee unboxes the device.

2. Employee runs through the initial setup screen.

3. Employees are ready to get to work with all their apps and settings configured.

Now, let me clarify. This doesn't mean Mac admins don't have a role to play here or that Apple will magically take care of the setup process

---

[2] www.apple.com/business/it/

[3] www.apple.com/education/k12/it/

themselves. No, what it means is that the majority of the heavy lifting from a logical point of view occurs in the backend between ABM/ASM and your MDM solution.

Initial settings, configurations, apps to deploy, management data, group assignments, and several other important factors are set up and tweaked by Mac admins. Once both services are operating as intended and synchronizing, the work is complete from the IT side of the equation. It is from here that the user takes over to perform unboxing and initial setup.

Just how much a user must do is up to the Mac admin, as most of the setup process can be automated for the user. Additional considerations are applications that may be difficult to install or complex configurations that are required to meet security, privacy, and compliance needs – while still possible to automate – may require a heavier lift (at least initially) by IT.

The beauty of the zero touch process is that, unless needs change (and of course they will) the enrollment process is largely dependent on how much (or how little) IT wants the user to do. Think of it on a sliding scale, the less IT does, the more automation is required and vice versa. But believe me when I say that I got chills the first time I saw a brand-new device, right out of the box go from initial power on to fully configured and ready for the end-user to use in 20–30 mins. If I'm being honest, I still get this fuzzy feeling seeing that happen combined with the knowledge of knowing that tens of thousands of Apple devices I was tasked with provisioning are each going to end up the same way –each and every time – for each user without my having to wipe my brow hundreds of times while working on each one individually.

It's truly a thing of beauty and best of all, it's the future and a completely manageable solution developed by Apple and carried out by MDM solution providers end-to-end. No corner cutting, no need to reinvent the wheel or mess with complex hardware/software configurations that break right when you need them most – fast, secure, efficient, and simple device deployment that "*just works.*"

Summary

In this chapter, we learned how to be good to ourselves as IT and Mac admins. The value of investing in ourselves by building our knowledge and evolving skill sets so that we don't have to work as hard every single time.

From implementing zero touch deployments to put macOS devices in the hands of users faster to how integrating features and expanding functionality makes IT's job friendlier by massaging in features that are critical to device security, like app deployment and device configuration.

We also discussed how ongoing management across the modern computing landscape has changed, favoring mobile device management – in turn opening the doorway for automating workflows that help Mac admins manage macOS from anywhere in the world. Freeing IT from manually repetitive tasks and permitting them to focus on becoming the best they possibly can while delivering excellent user support, or as I like to call it, "working smarter, *not* harder."

CHAPTER 10

Have a Plan and Stick to It

Just like the previous chapter, this one is also aimed at budding IT professionals and Mac admins. Individual users on their personal devices could certainly benefit from some of the sections included in this chapter, but it will largely be applicable to administrators tasked with managing Apple at the enterprise level.

In a nutshell, the focus of this chapter will be on guidance and recommendations based on best practices, common sense, and anecdotal evidence to figure out the best solution to a problem by identifying the need, doing your research, hypothesizing what the best solution may be, testing it, and reviewing the results, while remaining as objective and pragmatic as possible to arrive at the best security solution to meet the needs of your organization, data, and users.

If this sounds a lot like a science experiment, well, that's because it's similar in a lot of ways. And no, you don't need a degree in science to conduct your testing of new strategies, applications, and solutions this way, just an organized approach that sees you testing out possibility objectively – removing personal bias whenever possible. In the end, the goal is to find the solution that will work best for your organization. Optimally, that solution will also be the one that works best with your style of management, therefore allowing the IT team, the organization, and its stakeholders to work more comfortably and efficiently, while enhancing security without compromising privacy.

© Jesus Vigo, Jr. 2023
J. Vigo, Jr., *Hardening Your Macs*, https://doi.org/10.1007/978-1-4842-8939-6_10

Standardize Your Environment

For a time in my IT career, I was part of a team of field-based administrators whose primary role involved standardizing locations that were operating outside of compliance parameters. We were meant to visit a location that was out of compliance and, through our combined efforts, standardize the entire IT operational structure at that location – we're talking from networking equipment to servers to computers, including implementing identity management based on directory services and network-based appliances running on-site, handling security for hundreds or thousands of devices and users depending on the size of the location.

Before I began that leg of my career, I was a Systems Administrator based out of a single location, supporting the environment by myself. As with any job role, colleagues leave, creating a hole that can take time to fill. In those cases, it is not uncommon for the remaining employees to "make ends meet" by shouldering more of a workload until the position is filled by a new candidate.

IT is no different in this sense. So, it was not an uncommon request for upper management to request that an administrator with greater experience be temporarily assigned to another location that currently is without their own admin to provide support where and when possible.

Having been requested to oversee several additional locations through my tenure, I quickly realized that if I'm to be as successful as an administrator at any new temporary locations as I was at the location I was mainly assigned to support (while still providing support for my main location as well, mind you) – I'm going to have to make a few changes that set me, and all the locations I'm responsible for, up for success.

Hence, the idea of standardizing environments as much as possible was born in my mind and I immediately took to the lab with a pen and a pad to identify the similarities between locations, highlight the differences, and brainstorm ideas to maximize security, while minimizing the impact to user productivity.

It wasn't easy at first and certainly there was push back from stakeholders. Partly because some solutions simply didn't mesh well. After all, as I've mentioned before, every organization will have differing needs and that will affect what will work and how it will function. The other part of the equation I chalked up to nothing more than difficulty in adopting new ways of doing things. For example, one location I was assigned to had a revolving door of administrators in the last five years prior to my taking over. It wasn't anyone's fault, just bad luck I suppose, but nonetheless, here I was.

Without getting too deep into specifics, there were a multitude of issues. But the biggest concern was that Macs were set up and configured according to the user they were assigned to. Some had necessary software installed, others hadn't been updated since the day they were powered on. Others had some security in place but almost all of them had administrator accounts with different passwords, selected by the individual that initially set it up. These were largely forgotten, and, in some instances, users refused to provide the admin-level credentials when requesting support.

All of this is to say that, while the reasoning may vary from one organization to the other, the process of standardization will always be a useful strategy to adjust processes so that they operate as expected each time. This, combined with baseline assessments, help organizations by running tests to determine the normal operating procedure of a device and/or network. When monitoring these devices, any time there is a deviation from the baseline or expected behavior, Mac admins are alerted to the fact that something is causing this behavior to be different and therefore, should be investigated to determine what the cause is and if it requires an adjustment to the baseline to account for the change or if it's a sign of a greater issue that requires remediation to correct. Thus, bringing your Mac back into compliance and within the usual operating parameters.

Develop Workflows to Address Common Issues

Part of creating and delivering automated solutions (which we'll go into in the next section) is tied most directly to workflows. Workflows are a grouping of processes that are used to resolve an issue or provide support for a request. Stated simply, it's what you as the administrator will do when a certain issue is identified.

Workflows can be developed to address any type of issue, let's make that clear. It's just significantly more difficult to establish a process that will resolve a solution when you're not familiar with it or have identified the root cause of the problem. Hence why I added the "address common issues" line to this section. Since common issues are replicable and so you know exactly what causes it and therefore, exactly what will resolve it.

Moreover, workflows aren't just for resolving issues, they are also for determining the best course of action when performing a task. Properly created and detailed workflows take the guesswork out of "how do I fix this?" or "what do I do next?" – think of them as blueprints that provide step-by-step instructions on how to perform a task. If you follow the steps, it'll work out the same way each time.

You may be thinking, why spend my time trying to develop workflows when that time could be better spent actually resolving issues instead of thinking up ways to resolve them? There's a certain logic in that and certainly, you will encounter situations where you've no time to spare in thinking up solutions – you just need to get in there and resolve it quickly.

At the same time, not every situation will require such haste and ultimately, the time spent on developing quality workflows will pay dividends each and every time that issue comes up. Think of it in terms of saving pennies but spending dollars. A properly developed workflow offers a solution and does so with maximum efficiency in mind – not additional time wasted.

Say, for example, you're tasked with configuring a Mac for a specific use case. It requires several device configurations for additional security for members of the sales team that frequently travel. Each time this comes up, your existing process is to manually login to the Mac, install Apple Configurator 2 and painstakingly create each configuration by hand, before handing the device back to the user. Let's assume that this process takes you 30 mins to perform per device but each time the request comes in, you must configure ten devices, one for each member of the sales team. And requests come in twice a month. That's a total of 300 mins per request – 600 mins per month – totaling five hours per session and ten hours per month.

Yet, if a workflow was developed in which the administrator created the device configurations once, then exported them to a location on a server, this would save a lot of time by eliminating the manual processes of downloading AC2 and creating the configurations ten times per session. This workflow could further be transformed by creating a basic Bash script that when executed, gathers the files from the server and installs each of the .mobileconfig payloads on the device. By doing this, the Mac admin has now eliminated the manual installation process as well, cutting down considerably more time.

Basically, this scenario has now been whittled down to roughly logging in manually and executing the script from the server. Even typing slowly, this would require a generously estimated five mins per device, resulting in 50 mins per session (less than one hour) or 100 mins per month (under two hours).

This example is intended to demonstrate the very real benefit to developing workflows and what that translates to for IT pros and Mac admins in terms of saving time, productivity, and efficiency. While this example doesn't reflect the kind of savings to expect from every scenario, it does illustrate the benefit rather accurately.

Just imagine what you could accomplish with an entire workday or even a couple of hours given back to you? It's an incredible feeling being able to work smarter, not harder. The key is to find workflows that balance security with how *you* work best. Those that work with your style as opposed to against it tend to be the best fit I've found.

Automate Whenever Possible

Going back to the scenario laid out in the previous section, what if I told you that the rough workflow sketched out in that section could be further refined, to the point that it would happen free of manual configuration? No help desk ticket required because the user would already receive their device configured as they need it from day one.

That is the power of automation. Whether it relies on the same script you created and utilizes a launch daemon[1] – a process in macOS that permits the creation of agents that will automatically launch or kick off events configured by administrators – or better still, becomes part of your MDM management workflow.

By incorporating it as part of the latter, when Mac devices are initially enrolled in the MDM, logic can be applied so that devices that are part of a particular group receive certain software and configured settings. Furthermore, using policies to ensure compliance, means when a trigger is detected, say connecting the Mac to a network that is not the corporate one, the policy executes the workflow to verify that the Mac belonging to a sales team member has the exact configuration required. If not, it triggers a secondary workflow to install the necessary configurations on affected devices, bringing them back into compliance.

---

[1] https://developer.apple.com/library/archive/documentation/MacOSX/ Conceptual/BPSystemStartup/Chapters/CreatingLaunchdJobs.html

Another example of the benefits of automation can be found in the Zero Touch section located in Chapter 9. In that section, we touched upon how zero touch is enabled by synchronizing your MDM solution with ABM/ASM.

When a new Mac is purchased from Apple or one of its authorized resellers, the device's serial number is automatically added to the list of company-owned devices in ABM/ASM. By integrating the data in ABM/ASM with your MDM, new device record placeholders are then added to your MDM's console where IT can add them to enrollment profiles. These enrollment profiles ensure two things:

1. When the device is powered on, it will automatically supervise the Mac upon enrollment with the MDM solution.

2. Upon enrollment, the device record is added to the MDM, allowing IT to manage security settings on Mac through configurations, installing patches, deploying apps, and enforcing compliance through policies.

Depending on the needs of the organization, Mac admins can vary, well automate most if not all of the management aspects for their Apple fleet right from their preferred MDM solution.

Stay on Top of the Latest Security Threats

This sort of reminds me of the saying "a solution in search of a problem." Keeping up to date with the newest security updates is one thing, but staying abreast of the latest security threats is a different beast altogether. Not because it's impossible, but rather because there are several threats in the wild (these are currently in use by bad actors). Of this type, there may or may not be patches available. There are those that are found by security researchers that have yet to be disclosed publicly (those that are possible but not being actively used). Similarly, there are those that are detected by researchers and made available to the public (this is one of the worst scenarios because developers in these cases find out when everyone else does, so usually there is no patch available as bad actors scramble to weaponize the threat). Then there are zero-day threats, these are unique in that they are not known, often referencing vulnerabilities that are so new that patches are not available and sometimes, few if any real workarounds available to minimize exposure to the threat.

Software updates provided by Apple are released regularly as issues are detected, tested, and finally, made available for public use. The best way to stay in the know with these is to check with Apple's Security Update Support Website.[2]

This site is frequently updated with the latest information on Apple software updates, specifically those relating to macOS, iOS, and first-party software across the entire Apple ecosystem. This information is kept in a hierarchical manner, with the most recent versions of updates found at the top of the page, then older updates listed as you scroll down. Toward the bottom, there are handy links where archived update records are kept year over year.

The best part about this website is that each update provided by Apple is included alongside pertinent data, such as release date, which OS and/ or device it pertains to, and a link to more detailed information providing a deep dive into what exactly the update does. Also, what threats and vulnerabilities are patched, which CVEs – if any – are remediated and not only what the threats do, but also who reported them in a categorized, organized fashion.

If checking the Apple website for updates is not your speed, try navigating to System Preferences | Software Update whenever you spot the small red badge on the top-right corner of the System Preferences icon in

---

[2] https://support.apple.com/en-us/HT201222

the dock. This visual alert notifies the user that a new update is available. By visiting the preference pane, any pending updates will be listed along with a brief description of what it does and a link to view more detailed information. Additionally, more recent versions of macOS will also display notifications when system updates are ready, taking users to the same preference pane to install it.

Now say you wish to stay better informed as to new and evolving security threats in general – which I highly recommend you do – there is no one specific place to do so. Rather, there are a number of different websites, RSS feeds, and lists to subscribe to that will provide a wealth of information relating to the state of cybersecurity. It's more of a personal preference how deeply you wish to dive into these waters, as there's definitely no lack of data out there for security-related matters.

Here are a few of the ones that I've used in the past to stay on-top of security threats looming over the horizon. But note, some of these are more security in general while others tend to be more focused on specific operating systems, like macOS.

- U.S. Cybersecurity and Infrastructure Security Agency (CISA) – Current Activity[3]

- Federal Bureau of Investigation (FBI) – Cybercrime news and press releases[4]

- Dark Reading[5]

- Objective-See[6]

---

[3] www.cisa.gov/uscert/ncas/current-activity
[4] www.fbi.gov/investigate/cyber/news
[5] www.darkreading.com
[6] https://objective-see.org/index.html

- Threat Post[7]

- Security Week[8]

- Cybersecurity News[9]

Additionally, here are a few podcasts that provide excellent accounts and background information of attacks that have occurred in the past, providing listeners great insight into the mindset of attackers. You can find these wherever you prefer listening to podcasts.

- Darknet Diaries

- DEF CON

- Malicious Life

Train Yourself (and Users) to Recognize Threats

I'm a big believer in continuing education (CE). And as a technologist, IT professional, Mac admin, or any such role involving cybersecurity or technology, it is in your best interest to believe in and abide by CE too.

I'm not referring specifically to enrolling in higher-education courses toward a graduate degree – though that's certainly part of it. I mean anything that adds educational value to your life as an administrator. Whether it's attending an instructor-led course, self-studying as part of a certification exam, reading up on the latest security threats, attending IT- and Security-focused events or even just networking with colleagues – each of these adds value by enriching your knowledge base, extending

---

[7] https://threatpost.com
[8] www.securityweek.com
[9] https://cybersecuritynews.com

your skill set or at the very least, adding a few more wrinkles to your brain than you had before you started.

Unpopular opinion: school is not for everyone. I'm not saying to give up on your dream of going to school – hell no! Quite the opposite, go after it with everything you've got. But realize that there are opportunities out there that exist far beyond the scope of pre- and post-graduate degrees specifically as it relates to security.

Be hungry, always learning and if there's something you don't understand, be relentless on your quest to figure it out. While I'm a firm believer that sometimes things happen for a reason and play out – not when we want them to – but more so *when* they need to happen as that's sometimes when they'll be appreciated the most.

By this, I do not mean to sit comfortably (or uncomfortably) on your laurels until something happens to you. You definitely *should* take the initiative to make things happen for yourself. This isn't a "you against the world" pep talk. It's just to say that initiative could mean working multiple jobs to pay for school for one person, while for the other it simply means not being fearful of asking the right person for help – each of those scenarios demonstrates different levels of initiative at play – but make no mistake, initiative it is.

At the risk of sounding prescriptive or the proverbial "finger wagging," I say this with hat firmly in hand as someone that always sought to "figure it out" when encountering something I didn't quite understand or committed myself to studying, researching, testing, and managing the latest technologies from Apple and other developers. I worked hard to learn each and every skill I hold, paying for courses, hours upon hours spent self-studying and taking and passing dozens of certification exams to verify my skills. All this while I worked different full-time IT roles throughout my career...eventually deciding to go and earn a Bachelor of Science in Cybersecurity and Information Assurance during the pandemic.

What I'm trying to say is that there are means out there. Sources of information that are ready, willing, and able to help. Don't lose sight of that.

Here are a few places to help those wishing to learn more about security get a foothold on their path:

- **CompTIA:** Non-profit organization that provides globally recognized training and certifications to IT professionals in a variety of disciplines.

- **EC-Council:** Globally recognized training and certifications aimed specifically at cybersecurity roles and paths.

- **Pearson IT:** A leader in IT certification learning solutions, from software-based learning tools to educational materials spanning a number of different disciplines, technologies and industry names.

- **Apress Books:** Publisher of books and training materials dedicated to the needs of IT professionals across many disciplines.

- **Apple Training:** Training and certification for Apple by Apple with flexible courses and in-depth courseware.

- **Community Colleges:** Many offer affordable courses, on campus and online, from entry-level IT to more specialized topics, like networking and security.

- **Western Governors University (WGU):** Online-only university that offers courses to obtain certifications and degree programs in various aspects of cybersecurity.

- **Cybersecurity Conferences (Local):** Smaller scale events designed to foster networking among IT professionals, obtain training and make connections.

- **Black Hat:** Cybersecurity convention held annually around the world showcasing seminars, discussions, and panels related to computer security.

- **DEF CON:** Cybersecurity convention held annually around the world showcasing seminars, discussions, and panels related to computer security.

Though many of the training and CE opportunities highlighted previously are open to users of all levels, the fact is that you've got to really like cybersecurity to be effective in it. For some, it's a perfect fit. For others, like casual users, they only want to know enough to protect themselves from making a bad decision – and that's a fair point.

Hence why part of the role of being an administrator includes a bit of training, whether you're training users, members of your team, or even a friend. Pass on what you have learned, educate them as you have been educated to protect them against the threats that are most prevalent to them. For example, the average end user probably wouldn't benefit much from knowing how to perform forensic investigations on a Mac. Unless that's their job role, it won't add much value to anyone outside IT and Security teams. Now, teaching end users about the dangers of phishing, how it works, what to look for and how to bypass those threats without clicking on links or giving up information, well, that could make the difference between their data staying free from harm or having to take their Mac to an actual forensic investigator to determine the extent of the threat that attacked their computer.

Lastly, there are a number of excellent services that provide this level of user training in an on-going capacity. Going so far as to integrate with your organization's existing infrastructure, like email, allowing IT to "test" user's knowledge on spotting threats and gauging their responses to customize training as necessary.

Align with Security Frameworks

Throughout this book, the topic of frameworks has been brought up in several chapters covering several topics. To recap, frameworks are a form of carefully designed blueprints that provide organizations formal guidance on how to best implement a particular app, policy, or strategy, based on best practices.

In the case of macOS security, several different frameworks exist from a variety of expert sources whose aim is to aid in securing your Apple computers to the highest degree possible. Similarly, some of the more robust frameworks also allow organizations to meet certain compliance levels that may be necessary to maintain a minimal level of adherence with data due to industry and/or regional regulations or laws.

Lastly, frameworks provide foundational stability and reliability that merely cobbling together security technologies to protect against macOS-centric threats may simply not address. Think of it as a map to get your organization's security practices and processes where you need them to go.

As mentioned, there are several different types of frameworks that focus on security. The general aim is not to adopt each and every framework to fortify your Mac fleet, but rather to choose one and stick to it. In some cases, you may need to select several, depending on your needs. For example, if your organization develops its own internal software, the security of your app may benefit from adopting the ESF for app development guidance in combination with the mSCP for securing macOS endpoints.

I'm going to highlight some of the more common ones while providing information related to each of their strengths in aiding and guiding your organization to endpoint security success.

- **Apple macOS security framework**[10]: Native to macOS, the security framework is designed by Apple to protect information, establish trust, and control access to software. This pertains to tools built in to macOS that secure resources and the configurations permitted to secure data, such as enabling the Firewall and enforcing FileVault.

- **Apple macOS privacy framework**[11]: Also developed by Apple, the aim of this framework is similar to its security relative, except it focuses primarily on achieving security through preserving user privacy. This controls how user data is accessed and used by apps and resources built-in to macOS, such as TCC and App Tracking Transparency (ATT).

- **Apple endpoint security framework (ESF)**[12]: Though it may sound eerily similar to the first framework on this list, it is different in that this framework is actually an API created by Apple to aid macOS app and service developers when designing software that monitors system events for potentially malicious behavior or suspicious activity.

- **National Institute of Standards and Technology (NIST) SP 800-179**[13]: The NIST is a part of the U.S. Department of Commerce that conducts research, authors technical papers, and offers guidance for a host

---

[10] https://developer.apple.com/documentation/security

[11] https://developer.apple.com/app-store/user-privacy-and-data-use/

[12] https://developer.apple.com/documentation/endpointsecurity

[13] https://csrc.nist.gov/publications/detail/sp/800-179/rev-1/archive/2018-10-19

of IT-related fields. Specifically, the SP 800 series of documentation provides industries and organizations expert guidance on how to implement and manage cybersecurity protocols successfully, tailoring content to specific OS's, industries, and use cases. The SP 800-179 document is no longer updated in favor of the newer partnership resulting in SP 800-219 forming the macOS Security Compliance Project (covered a little later).

- **Center for Internet Security (CIS) Apple macOS benchmarks**[14]: The CIS benchmark is an objective security guideline that provides consensus-driven guidance derived from experts in the Apple macOS community and provides a step-by-step checklist of optimal configurations to secure your Mac.

- **macOS security compliance project (mSCP)**[15]: An open-source effort that extends the work of the NIST SP 800-179 by partnering with National Aeronautics and Space Administration (NASA), Defense Information Systems Agency (DISA) and Los Alamos National Laboratory (LANL) to customize security baselines for macOS security controls that are mapped to compliance requirements.

- **Department of Defense (DoD) Defense Information Systems Agency (DISA) Apple macOS Security Technical Implementation Guide (STIG)**[16]: A configuration standard developed by the DoD that

---

[14] www.cisecurity.org/benchmark/apple_os

[15] https://github.com/usnistgov/macos_security

[16] https://public.cyber.mil/announcement/stig-update-disa-releases-the-apple-macos-12-security-technical-implementation-guide/

consists of cybersecurity requirements for macOS to secure protocols within Mac, including networking, hardware, software, physical, and logical architectures to strengthen security and preserve privacy while reducing vulnerabilities.

Comply with Regulatory Requirements

The previous section on security frameworks and these go rather hand in hand due to adopting certain frameworks that can help organizations to configure their Mac computers for compliance, while also verifying that they are indeed compliant.

Also, a solid MDM solution that allows customized integration with third-party software solutions can also provide administrators an edge in verifying macOS device compliance with regulatory requirements by incorporating the results from a framework, like mSCP, for example, that's been set for a particular compliance level.

The output provided from mSCP is configured for say, Systems and Organization Controls (SOC) 2 compliance. This certification is the result of an audit of an organization's internal controls over information systems and the users of those services to determine if they meet the various criteria required to achieve the designation. As an aside, SOC 2 is not a requirement for all organizations and could very well be something your company never has to achieve. On the other hand, perhaps your organization is governed by industry and/or governmental regulations and laws that specifically require this type of assurance be implemented and maintained in order to continue conducting business in that industry and/or region.

In those cases, a framework as stated before provides administrators and company stakeholders the step-by-step guidance necessary to achieving their regulatory goals and maintain them as part of the requirement.

For clarity, just because your organization does not require adherence to a certain type of regulation does not mean that securing macOS should just be considered some half-measured approach. Companies still work with critical, sensitive, and often proprietary data that, while not regulated per se, is not necessarily something the company would wish (or sometimes even afford) to have this data made publicly available. Hence, the variety of security frameworks that exist to secure macOS and meet your organizational security needs.

It is difficult to quantify what regulation(s) your company may be subject to, given the impossibility of me possibly knowing each company, what industry they perform in, where they're located, and what their processes are relating to data gathering, management, and storage. Simply put, each case could present a set of unique and variably different requirements, calling for multiple solutions.

No to mention that each company has their own financial take on the matter, some choosing to "go it alone" while others have the capital to hire partners with experience in achieving certification status for different regulations and/or in different regions. So, your mileage may vary, is what I'm saying.

Frameworks help organizations meet compliance requirements, but the on-going management required to ensure that devices stay that way is a different process altogether. One that requires practices and workflows tailored to monitor, identify, and remediate issues detected to bring devices back into compliance.

An example of this was used previously when discussing policies in Chapter 9, in the Securing Devices section. When discussing the example for DLP, this is a perfect scenario of compliance enforcement. For example, say you're working for a healthcare provider and tasked with implementing HIPAA compliance for medical professionals that travel. HIPAA makes provisions stating that medical records cannot be shared without the prior authorization of the patient – this applies if data is lost or stolen, as well.

So, if a doctor that performs home visits tests a number of patients and records their vitals to their medical records on a MacBook Pro laptop, it is part of that regulation to ensure that the records are only accessible by the doctor and medical staff. Should the laptop get stolen, and a bad actor is able to copy the medical records and sell them on the dark web, that would result in several violations to HIPAA, resulting in a costly fine to the doctor and perhaps the organization that employs them.

If the device has encryption enabled, however, it would be rather difficult for the bad actor to defeat the encryption, keeping the records safe. Furthermore, the DLP provision goes deeper to protect the confidential patient records, making it so that if data was to be copied to an external source, DLP would catch this attempt and effectively block it from occurring, again keeping data safe and out of the hands of unauthorized users in line with HIPAA's regulatory provisions.

Design a Defense In-Depth Plan

You may have heard the term "defense in depth" bandied about or mentioned here within the pages of this book in earlier chapters. To ascertain what a defense in-depth plan is you must first need to understand the requirements of securing macOS within your organization. This includes the various nuances to your Mac fleet, how devices are used, when and where, and by whom.

It's also critical to develop an understanding of your pain points or the risk to the organization, how and where it comes from, as well as identifying the types of attacks that the organization is up against.

While it is a lot to take in, consider it as pieces of a larger puzzle. The more pieces you have, the clearer the picture will be, no? If you don't have all the pieces, that's ok too. That's essentially the crux of defense in depth, to design a security strategy or plan that combines multiple security controls, weaving them together, to effectively identify, prevent, and mitigate security threats affecting macOS, your users, and data.

Again, there is no silver bullet solution or one-size-fits-all that will stop all the threat types affecting your organization. Put another way, even if there was, you're now subject to a single point of failure, meaning that even if that one "all-magical" solution did exist and was protecting your entire Mac fleet, should it fail at any point or for any reason, your Apple devices are basically unprotected until this unicorn solution is active again.

I often equate defense in depth (DiD) with a cake. A large cake with multiple layers, each one representing a unique security solution. By "weaving" them together, I meant that they work in tandem with one another so that if one were to fail or permit something malicious to slip through, the subsequent security control would be there to catch it, stop it, or at the very least, alert IT and/or Security teams to its existence, allowing them to jump into action to take care of it before it leads to something way worse.

Let me illustrate this with an example before providing a list of security controls that should be on your organization's list of security protections as part of their defense in-depth plan.

Consider the following real-world scenario of a phishing attack carried out by a bad actor, looking to infect your Mac with ransomware, while pivoting access to find other devices on your network to infect as well. You have the following security controls in place:

- Content Filter

- Firewall

- Antivirus

- Data Backup

- User Training

1. The bad actor attempts to communicate with your Mac, but because the Firewall is configured to block any connections not previously allowed by IT, the connection is never established.

2. Let's say the Firewall lets the connection slip through for some odd reason and you receive the message with a suspicious link attached. The training you received informs you that this is not safe, and you decide to not click on the link and report it to IT.

3. But what if you ignored your training and did click the link? It would normally take you to a rogue website that downloads the malware and infects your Mac, but since there is a Content Filter configured, it knows that this is a phishing domain and blocks access to the website, preventing the malware from downloading.

4. Ok, the phishing domain was unknown to the filter and after you clicked on the link, it downloaded the malware, before immediately beginning the infection process. Luckily, you have antivirus installed on your Mac which identifies the threat by signature and prevents it from executing before removing the threat altogether from Mac.

5. Or did it? Instead of signature-based, let's say that it's a new piece of malware so it was allowed to execute, infecting your Mac and encrypting your data with ransomware. Game over, right? You either pay the ransom and hope to get the decryption key or forever lose your data. But then you remembered that you perform regular backups of your data, so while the data on your Mac may have fallen to ransomware encryption, the data on your backup drive is available and not affected by ransomware. Once your Mac is clean and remediated from malware, you only need to reconnect your backup drive to quickly restore any affected data.

The preceding is just one example of how an effective defense in-depth plan could work to keep your Mac, users, and data safe – not because each individual solution is so perfectly set that it stops everything that comes up against it. No, it's effective because – at the end of the day – multiple solutions were in place to catch a threat that could potentially be missed by a previous control because life isn't perfect and neither is technology, but having redundancies in place often helps to eliminate some if not most of the pitfalls, thus making security more effective, while keeping it manageable.

Mixing physical, technical, and administrative security controls are key when choosing which controls to consider in developing a modern DiD plan:

Physical

- Security guards
- Door locks
- Biometrics
- Man trap

- Key card access

- Cameras

- Cable locks

Technical

- Device management

- Patch management

- Endpoint security (Antivirus)

- Content filter

- Firewall

- Secure communications (ZTNA, VPN)

- Compliance enforcement

- Encryption

- Identity management

- Active monitoring

- Logging and auditing

- Threat hunting

Administrative

- User training

- Company policies

- Inventory management

- Risk assessment

- On-boarding processes

- Data handling procedures

- Security requirements

Summary

In this final chapter, we covered the importance of a well-structured, comprehensive plan and how it works to holistically strengthen the security of your Apple endpoints, while preserving user privacy to safeguard Mac, users, and of course, data.

Some would argue that it's impossible to account for everything and I tend to agree with that philosophy. It's exponentially difficult to conceive of each possible pain point and account for them in general, let alone when taking into account just how quickly technology advances. What's secure today, could be just less secure tomorrow…and in eighteen months, well, it could very well be outdated according to Moore's law – perhaps even obsolete.

The best we can hope for is to take a pragmatic, sensible approach to security by leveraging the tools, technology, and data available to us as administrators to develop a cohesive defense in-depth plan that targets as many conceivable threats as possible using a layered approach to cast the widest net possible when protecting macOS-based assets and resources.

Using the touch points included in this chapter, including standardizing your environment to develop workflows and automations that work for you – not against – is an excellent starting point. Keeping you and your stakeholders educated by informing yourselves of the latest threats and utilizing extensive training resources to not only take your skills to the next level but keep them razor sharp is an excellent way to maintain them. Lastly, using these resources in combination with the detailed information found within this book, you can develop and implement a comprehensive defense in depth plan that serves your organization, its stakeholders, and you. One that effectively minimizes risk, mitigating against the latest threats, and iteratively fortifies your Apple infrastructure by aligning with established security frameworks to comply with organizational, governmental, and/or regional regulatory requirements.

Index

A

Apple devices, 5, 8, 28, 42, 53
    configuration, 184
    distribution, 58
    external security
        protections, 83–95
    frameworks, 59
    hardware, 56
    iCloud services, 126
    internal vectors, 97
    macOS devices, 64
    MDM services, 182
    security, 200
    software, 57, 58
Apple remote desktop (ARD), 179
Apps/packages deployment, 185, 186
Automate workflows, 188, 189
Automation, 199, 200

B

Baseline assessments, 195

C

Center for Internet
    Security (CIS), 208
Comprehensive plan, 216
Computer security, *see* Security
Content delivery network (CDN),
    132, 133
Continuing education (CE), 202–205

D

Data Loss Prevention (DLP), 188,
    210, 211
Defense in depth (DiD)
    administrative, 215
    designing plan, 211
    physical controls, 214
    security protections, 212, 213
    technical controls, 215
Defense Information Systems
    Agency (DISA), 208
Denial of service (DoS), 38

Department of Defense (DoD), 208

Device configuration, 183–185, 192, 197

Distributed Denial of Service (DDoS), 38

E

Endpoint security framework (ESF), 137, 145, 206, 207

External security protections

accessories, 90–92

booting option, 84

cable lock, 88

components, 84

docking stations/privacy screens, 91

external storage devices/input devices, 91

Intel processors, 83

licensed cables, 93, 94

password (Intel-based Mac), 85

sensor covers, 90

smart card readers/webcam covers, 92

system's startup, 83

volume-level encryption, 86–88

wireless devices, 91

F

FileVault, 88–90, 135

internal vectors, 111–114

Filtering technology, 187

Firewall technology, 119–122

Flat packages, 185

G

Graphical user interface (GUI), 53, 142–147, 160, 162, 179, 184

H

Hardening process

attack surface, 74, 75

definition, 71

encryption equals, 72

nutshell, 73

security-based processes, 72

software (macOS)/hardware (Mac computer), 72

vectors, 75–77, 80

vulnerability, 78

workarounds, 77–81

I, J, K

iCloud services

data security, 127

deep integration, 130

DNS records and IP address, 128

email privacy, 129

end-to-end encryption, 127

features, 126

Keychain, 128

Mac command, 173

Mac devices, 131
management option, 130
recovering/access policies, 127
2FA, 127
Indicators of Compromise (IoC), 37
Information Technology (IT), 5
administrators, 106, 121
career, 177–191
industry, 17
professionals, 143, 193–215
security teams, 108
shadow IT, 36
Internal vectors
administrator password, 104
extensions, 167–169
file and folder
permissions, 145–156
binary notation, 154
chmod command, 152
desktop operation, 147
grouping files, 150
modification, 146
octal notation, 153, 155
respective permissions, 154
symbolic notation, 149, 152
user accounts and security
groups, 148
warning message, 148
FileVault, 111–114
firewall technology, 119–122
gatekeeper, 118
hibernation, 135
iCloud (see iCloud services)
iCloud resources, 109

lock screen, 115, 116
login, 102
Mac App Store, 132–134
malware protection, 116–119
multifactor
authentication, 108–110
notarization, 117
passwords
Keychain Access, 100
modifications, 98
requirement, 113
2FA, 100
warnings, 97, 98
remote wipe, 172–174
screen saver, 113–115
secure virtual memory,
134–136
security functions, 113
sharing preference
pane, 156–166
SIP technology, 166
software-based
technologies, 116
software update
capabilities, 141–144
system preferences, 103, 104
TCC controls, 136–139
technological and feature
settings, 97
third-party applications,
144, 145
time machine, 169–171
Touch ID's technology, 139–141
user accounts, 104–108

Internal vectors (*cont.*)
  virtual private networking,
    122, 123
  XProtect, 117
  zero trust, 123–126

L

Low-Level Bootstrap (LLB), 61

M

Mac App Store, 44, 58, 132–134,
    142, 144, 158, 167, 168, 184
Mac devices
  administration, 193–215
macOS devices, 41, 99, 101
  ACME products, 50
  act process, 46–48
  Apple's Frameworks, 59
  automation, 198, 199
  components, 49
  developer kits, 63
  distribution, 58
  extension, 168
  extensions, 168
  FileVault, 62
  gatekeeper, 62
  hardware, 56
  iCloud private relay, 66
  internal vectors, 140
  knowledge is power, 41
  MacBook Pro, 42

memory protection engine, 62
motivations, 47–49
network/security
    technologies, 63
NeXTSTEP operating system, 55
privacy, 64–66
remote controls, 178–192
scenarios, 44
secure device management, 63
security, 43, 60, 206
simplicity, 57
software, 57, 58
software-based security
    protections, 61, 62, 64
T2 security chip, 60
UEFI firmware security, 61
user data protections, 62
XProtect, 62
macOS security compliance project
    (mSCP), 206, 208, 209
Malware removal tool (MRT),
    63, 117
Man-in-the-middle (MitM), 20,
    22, 35, 187
Meta packages, 185
Mobile device management
    (MDM), 112, 113, 133, 145,
    180–184, 186–191, 198,
    199, 209
Moore's law, 216
Multifactor authentication (MFA),
    108–110, 125

N, O

NeXTSTEP operating system, 55

P, Q

Personal computer (PC),
8, 53, 105
Personally Identifiable
Information (PII), 73, 74

R

Regulatory requirements,
209–211, 216
Remote control shares, 178–180
Risk assessment
appetite and tolerance, 23, 24
assessment, 15–17
concepts, 13
device types, 15
matrices, 18–23
risk, 14, 15
tolerance, 24
vectors, 76

S

Security, 4
definition, 6, 7
elements, 3
frameworks, 206–209
hardware-and software-based
protections, 5
history, 8–10

legitimate and illegitimate
reasons, 3
mitigate risk and resolve
problems, 4
operating systems, 201
podcasts, 202
posture, 10
privacy, 60
responsibilities, 11, 12
software updates, 199
system preferences, 200
threats, 43
tools and frameworks, 186–188
trivial/inconsequential, 9
Wi-Fi hotspot, 4
Security Technical Implementation
Guide (STIG), 208
Sharing preference pane
AirPlay receiver, 166
Apple events, 164
bluetooth, 165
content caching, 165
control access, 156–166
directories, 160
file and folder permissions, 159
file sharing service, 160
internet access, 164
media service, 163
printers section, 163
remote management, 164
screen sharing, 158
services, 156, 157
system preferences, 161
terminal information, 162

Signed system volume (SSV), 61
Standardizing environments,
    194, 195
System integrity protection (SIP),
    62, 166–167
System on a Chip (SoC), 60
Systems and Organization
    Controls (SOC), 209

T

Threats
    attacks, 31–33
    attack vector, 28
    CE, 202–205
    communication, 29
    data exfiltration, 34
    definition, 27
    external category, 37–39
    internal/external attacks, 33–36
    Mac, 30
    malware/eavesdropping
        types, 30
    MitM, 35
    passcode/biometrics
        solution, 29
    security, 199, 201
    shoulder surfing, 36
    social engineering, 36
    suspicious websites, 31
    theft/loss, 35
    unauthorized access/rouge
        accessories, 30

    unauthorized devices, 36
    vulnerabilities, 28
Time machine, 169–171
Touch ID's technology, 61, 103,
    115, 116, 139–141
Transparency, consent and control
    (TCC), 62, 64, 119, 136–139
Two-Factor Authentication (2FA),
    100, 108–110, 127

U

Unified Extensible Firmware
    Interface (UEFI), 61, 83

V

Vector identification, 75–77
Virtual Network Computing (VNC),
    158, 164, 178, 179
Virtual Private Networking (VPN),
    20, 43, 44, 122–123, 125, 215
Volume-level encryption, 86–88

W, X, Y

Western Governors University
    (WGU), 204
Workflow development, 196–198

Z

Zero touch, 182, 189–192, 199
Zero Trust, 123–126, 187

Printed in the United States
by Baker & Taylor Publisher Services